Chakras for Beginners

The Newcomer's Guide to Awakening and Balancing Chakras. Radiate Positive Energy Others Will Notice. Includes a Spiritual Guide to Essential Oils, Gems and Herbs for Meditation and Healing.

Kara Lawrence

© Copyright 2020 - All rights reserved.

The content contained within this book may not be reproduced, duplicated or transmitted without direct written permission from the author or the publisher.

Under no circumstances will any blame or legal responsibility be held against the publisher, or author, for any damages, reparation, or monetary loss due to the information contained within this book, either directly or indirectly.

Legal Notice:

This book is copyright protected. It is only for personal use. You cannot amend, distribute, sell, use, quote or paraphrase any part, or the content within this book, without the consent of the author or publisher.

Disclaimer Notice:

Please note the information contained within this document is for educational and entertainment purposes only. All effort has been executed to present accurate, up to date, reliable, complete information. No warranties of any kind are declared or implied. Readers acknowledge that the author is not engaged in the rendering of legal, financial, medical or professional advice. The content within this book has been derived from various sources. Please consult a licensed professional before attempting any techniques outlined in this book.

By reading this document, the reader agrees that under no circumstances is the author responsible for any losses, direct or indirect, that are incurred as a result of the use of the information contained within this document, including, but not limited to, errors, omissions, or inaccuracies.

Table of Contents

INTRODUCTION 1

CHAPTER 1: EMBRACE YOUR CHAKRAS 7

WHAT ARE CHAKRAS, EXACTLY - ANOTHER LOOK 8
   A Brief History of Chakras 8
   How Chakras Influence Us in Our Daily Lives 11
   Understanding Chakra Energy 12
WHAT IT MEANS TO BE OUT OF BALANCE 13
WHAT IT MEANS TO BE IN BALANCE 16
   How to Achieve Balance 17
   Which Chakra Do I Start With? 19

CHAPTER 2: YOUR ROOT 21

COLORS AND SYMBOLS 22
IS YOUR ROOT OFF-BALANCE? 24
   Symptoms of an Off-Balance Root 25
   Why Healing Your Root Is Important 27
   Open Your Root 29

CHAPTER 3: YOUR SACRAL CHAKRA 35

COLORS AND SYMBOLS 36
CHECKING YOUR SACRAL CHAKRA FOR BALANCE 39
OPEN YOUR SACRAL CHAKRA 42

CHAPTER 4: YOUR SOLAR PLEXUS 49

COLORS AND SYMBOLS 52
THE IMPORTANCE OF BALANCE IN THE SOLAR PLEXUS 53
OPENING YOUR SOLAR PLEXUS 57

CHAPTER 5: YOUR VERY HEART 61

COLORS AND SYMBOLS OF THE HEART 63

KEEPING YOUR HEART IN BALANCE 65
    Open and Breathe 68

CHAPTER 6: YOUR THROAT 71

  SYMBOLS AND COLORS 72
  BALANCE IN YOUR THROAT: WHAT TO STRIVE FOR, AND SIGNS OF
  BLOCKAGE 74
  OPEN AND SPEAK 78

CHAPTER 7: YOUR THIRD EYE 83

  SYMBOLS AND COLORS 85
  KEEPING YOUR THIRD EYE WIDE OPEN 87
    Awaken 92

CHAPTER 8: YOUR CROWN CHAKRA 95

  SYMBOLS AND COLORS 97
  YOUR CROWN: A FLAWED GEM 99
  SEATING YOUR CROWN 103

CHAPTER 9: BALANCE AND HEAL YOUR CHAKRAS 107

  CHAKRA TRIAGE 107
    Results 110
  HOW TO HEAL 111
    Meditation 111
    Affirmations 115
    Yoga 118
    Diet 125
    Reiki 128
    Emotional Freedom Technique (EFT) 130

CHAPTER 10: BOOST YOUR HEALING - THE SPIRITUAL GUIDE TO CRYSTALS, HERBS AND ESSENTIAL OILS 133

  CRYSTALS AND GEMS 133
    A Rule of Thumb 134
    Smoky Quartz (Root) 135
    Hematite (Root) 135
    Carnelian Agate (Sacral) 136
    Gold Tiger Eye (Solar Plexus) 136

- *Rose Quartz (Heart)* 137
- *Celestite (Throat)* 139
- *Azurite (Third Eye)* 139
- *Amethyst (Crown)* 140
- HERBS AND ESSENTIAL OILS 141
  - *Essential Oils* 141
  - *Herbs* 146

CONCLUSION 151

REFERENCES 155

Introduction

"There is deep wisdom within our very flesh, if we can only come to our senses and feel it." - Elizabeth A. Behnke (Wise Old Sayings, 2020)

Consider your nervous system. It's a network of conduits sending signals from your brain across your body and back again, allowing every organ in each system to work together in harmony for optimum health and performance. We are taught in high school that our nervous system manages to do all this through electrical impulses, and then due to curriculum and time constraints we don't go any deeper. We don't explore the implications of what this could mean.

This book is about Chakras, that much is obvious. But what even *is* a Chakra exactly? Is it an accessory to a baloney sandwich? Is it a fad to go with a hipster's fedora? Or is there something more to it?

The earliest surviving record of the term *Chakra* derives from ancient Vedic Sanskrit texts, where it was first posited that we contain wheels, or *Cakram*, of power and energy within our bodies. These texts speculated on there being over a hundred Chakras throughout the human form, but made reference to seven primary Chakras. These seven Chakras tend to be what we think of when we hear the term and include the Crown, Third

Eye, Throat, Heart, Solar Plexus, Sacral, and the Root Chakras.

These seven are thought to run down along our head and spine, with the Root Chakra at the base of our spine, and the Crown at the very top of our head.

Although the idea of "energy wheels" being present in our body might sound mystical, modern medicine shows that our head and our spine - the places where our seven main Chakras reside - are the locations for our central nervous system. Different points of the central nervous system then branch out into the peripheral nervous system, much like how the main Chakras were said to break off into "rivers" that flow into our smaller Chakras. This is where things begin to get interesting.

Chakras, then, are a lens through which the ancients understood the nervous system and its relationship with the rest of the body. Likewise, this book aims to impart to you the knowledge needed to tap into their thoughts and techniques, at least at a basic level. Why is this important?

Consider what happens when your nervous system is impaired in some way. When you are drunk, your nerves send signals more slowly to one another. This means the rate at which you're able to react to the world around you slows down, making you come off as uncoordinated, sluggish, or bizarre to outside observers. It can even cost you your life, all because you have a blockage or delay in your nervous system.

Likewise, how do you feel after a night of poor sleep? Maybe you feel irritable. Maybe you battle to concentrate. Maybe your muscles and bones even feel more stiff and achy than usual, without there being a clear reason why.

Even dehydration can cause delays, because all cells need water to operate efficiently, and that includes your nerve cells and especially your brain cells. This disruption in our energy signals, once again, leads to our body becoming easier to hurt, and our mind easier to anger and confuse (Heid, 2014).

Why does a disruption in our energy flow cause such drastic problems? Well, our body is full of glands. There are many glands in our body, but the *seven* main glands covered by our parasympathetic nervous system include pineal gland, pituitary gland, thyroid, thymus, adrenal gland, pancreas, and sex gland (ovaries for women, testes for men).

Most of these glands produce hormones that our body needs to function at all, and they all need to be produced at just the right amount for us to function properly. What determines whether or not our hormones get produced at the right time, in the right amount? The nerve signals - the flow of energy - from our brain, down our spine and through the rest of our body are responsible.

So, clearly it is important to look after our nervous system, which is our body's ability to let energy flow to where it is needed, when it is needed.

The concept of Chakras has been used for thousands of years as a way to further aid and improve the efficiency of your energy flow. The idea is that by keeping your seven main Chakras unblocked, energy will flow more freely and easily through your body and thereby improve its state of being.

This is important to know, as sometimes we feel a little "off" or have some unexplained bugbear that follows us around no matter how well we sleep, how much water we drink, or how great our diet is. Sometimes we know we aren't fulfilling one of those needs properly, but maybe do not have the luxury to do so. The examination of your Chakras, then, may be what you need to help you get your energy flow back on track.

Although some methods of clearing or healing a Chakra involve crystals, there are also methods that require nothing more than just the presence of your body and mind, and I'll be covering both of these angles and more as often as possible for each Chakra.

As you learn about each Chakra, you'll gain further insight into how they work, as well as practical advice for how you can aid your nervous system, and therefore your body as a whole, through checking up on them and clearing them, whether alone or with the aid of a professional healer.

If you've ever felt lonely, lost, disconnected, or vaguely ill, you'll find that as you work through your Chakras in each chapter, there will be a change. Like a bright soul shaking off a bad hangover, you'll find yourself stepping out of a malaise that previously seemed unshakable. And just as the drunk connects more deeply again with others after sobering, or the sleep-deprived arrives in a better mood after a good rest, you'll find that by improving your energy flow, no matter how well you connect with others now, you'll begin to emit a new and more powerful sense of self that others will notice, and perhaps even love.

Chapter 1:

Embrace Your Chakras

You are an energy being. Your entire lived experience is defined by your body's ability to communicate with itself through the pulses of electricity it sends through your entire being. In the introduction, we already touched on how our nervous system affects our hormone production, and how Chakras can be a relevant and useful lens for helping us self-diagnose and regulate this system. However, we haven't yet touched on how important it is to monitor our energy flow even outside the context of hormones.

It's been scientifically proven that our emotional stress can have measurable physiological impacts on our bodies (Hairston, 2019). When you're experiencing heartache or anxiety, your bodily cells are being damaged on a microscopic level. This is why grief can feel so exhausting; even though you haven't been actively moving much, your body has been tearing itself apart in response to the imbalance of your energy. Of course, periodic energy imbalances are natural (grief being a great example) but that doesn't mean you cannot use your Chakras to help make the most constructive use of these imbalances possible.

What Are Chakras, Exactly - Another Look

A Brief History of Chakras

While Western readers may most readily correlate Chakras with the glands attached to the parasympathetic nervous system, the concept of Chakras itself, and thus its older meanings, did not originate in the West and existed long before we had modern anatomical knowledge. This imbues Chakras with a rich collection of cultural histories.

In Indian belief, Chakras are not just biological energy centers with roots in anatomy, but are also a way for the soul to achieve greater union with the Divine. Out of the seven main Chakras we mentioned in the Introduction, three are considered "physical" (from the Root to the Solar Plexus) and three are considered "spiritual (from the Throat to the Crown), with one acting as the bridge between the two (the Heart). However, you will find that there's a great deal of overlap between them as our body, mind, and soul are all connected. They are not all isolated in separate boxes, but live and breathe together in a complementary manner.

Intriguingly, in the oldest traditional sources, we see that the ancients did not arrive at the idea of seven Chakras straight away. While their teachings were based on observation, a precursor to scientific enquiry, the lack of modern technology and investigation methods to delve into anatomy meant that for a long time there was much debate on how many "main" Chakras we actually had, with most sages believing there to be between five and eight. It was only as time went on that this number shrank to a more accurate 6-7, and then finally to a nearly definitive seven as this semi-mystical concept began to show correlations with other scientific ideas.

In China, where the concept emigrated to from India in ancient times, Chakras were once again associated with anatomy through being correlated with the practice of acupuncture, although once again there was a divine or mystical element as the Chinese believed opening the Chakras allowed a better flow of qi or chi, which not only stood for a person's life force, but also a way for them to commune with the Divine. Regardless of your own spiritual beliefs, you may find that tending to your

Chakras will allow you a closer relationship with your deity.

Even if you have no deity, tending your Chakras can bring you great stress relief through stimulating your Vagus nerve, which helps reduce anxiety and thus eliminate the plethora of health issues that tend to come with stress, such as inflammation, heart attack risk, and the like.

It should be clear by now that the beliefs around Chakras are not static or unchanging, but are a living, breathing collection of ideas that grow and evolve according to observation and practice. A person's knowledge of both spiritual and anatomical knowledge will inform and change the way they approach Chakras, although historically Chakras have had both a mundane *and* a sublime aspect associated with them.

In the modern age, the concept of Chakras holds merit not only among Tantric traditions in India or the practitioners of Chinese medicine, but they also find traction among the Himalayan Bonpo, who believe that Chakras hold the power to determine the quality of our experiences in life.

Among Western civilization, Chakras are finding increasing grip within New Age spiritual and religious groups, where it fulfills much the same function as it did for the ancients.

How Chakras Influence Us in Our Daily Lives

Among those who know of Chakras, it is commonly believed that each one governs a certain aspect of life or well-being above and beyond what we can logically infer through study of the nervous system. As an example, the Root Chakra, which is located at the base of our spine, is said to affect our ability to feel secure or recognize support, whereas the Crown Chakra (located at the top of your head) is associated with the ability to learn, to make effective decisions based on intuition rather than immediate data, as well as the ability to not lose sight of one's goals when presented with a tasty distraction.

Overall, Chakras play a huge role in our day-to-day lives. They react to our emotions, increasing or decreasing their intake or output of energy in response to our joy, our pleasure, our pain and our grief. Can you imagine what it must feel like, for instance, when your Root Chakra is put off-balance by a traumatic experience?

Life happens, and all the while these wheels of pure energy keep spinning, either pulling energy into our bodies through counterclockwise motion, or out of our bodies through clockwise motions. Whether we give or absorb energy depends on our own state of being; whether we give off an energizing or draining feeling to those around us depends on our own current well-being. Long-term attractiveness is therefore not just a matter of personality or charisma, but also of physical and mental well-being. The more your body needs to absorb energy, the stronger a person's energy output needs to be for them to connect with you. Likewise, the more energy you can put out, the more you can safely take on without feeling exhausted, whether that exhaustion is physical, mental, emotional, or spiritual.

How much energy you have to absorb or can put out, again, comes down to your Chakras. However, the state of your Chakras is never set in stone. Rather, they are ever-shifting in response to your own consciousness. Although your emotions can throw your Chakras off-balance, they can also be used to re-seat them and restore yourself to order.

Understanding Chakra Energy

Although there is some correlation with our physiology, Chakras themselves are not directly measurable. It's comparable to how in ancient times, especially before the Renaissance, you could not measure wind as a definitive numerical value but could still see its power through how it bends bamboo, or shifts tumbleweed. Likewise, Chakras are not directly measurable (at least, not yet), but their use nonetheless creates noticeable impacts in the rest of your physiology.

Harnessing Chakra energy, then, is a way for your consciousness to interface with your subconscious processes and, through this, make subtle corrections for the long-term benefit of your body, such as the reseating mentioned earlier. Therefore, correcting your Chakras not only helps your glands function better, but can also lower the chance of them going awry to begin with.

What it Means to be Out of Balance

But why do these corrections need to be made? Shouldn't our Chakras be self-regulating, just like the rest of our internal subconscious systems? Well, yes, of course! Our Chakras, much like the rest of our body, labor tirelessly to keep us healthy and in perfect working order. But if all our internal systems self-regulated perfectly, we'd never get sick, would we? We'd never develop cancer, we'd never have allergic reactions, and we'd never have mood swings brought about by physiological changes. Sometimes our subconscious needs higher guidance.

When we are ill in some way, we respond by making it better. This can mean taking medicine, but not always. For instance, a person suffering from depression or anxiety might choose to take up exercise in order to encourage the production of "feel-good" hormones to let them safely and naturally balance out their mindset and perk themselves up.

Our knowledge of Chakras, then, is our way of learning what "exercises" we can take up in order to balance ourselves out when something is amiss.

Previously, we described the way energy flows from our Chakras as little rivers and streams flowing to each corner of our body. However, the seven main Chakras themselves form a river. Running from the base of our spine to the top of our head, they form a mighty stream that best flows when it is free of blockages at every point.

The balance of each Chakra affects the other. For instance, if our Root Chakra, our center of security and support, feels "blocked," then our Sacral Chakra might try to go into overdrive in order to make up the difference. Chakras like being in balance, so each one has a habit of overworking itself if the body senses that another Chakra is lacking.

You'll remember that the Sacral Chakra comes just after the Root Chakra in terms of placement. What you might not know is that the Sacral is linked to one's sexuality, passion, and creativity. So, in this example, what do you think might happen if our Root Chakra does not have enough energy flow through it, and the Sacral Chakra tries to make up the difference?

If you've ever heard of the term "rebound sex," it's closely linked to this. All of our Chakras are affected by our emotions and state of mind, but our Chakras can also affect these things in turn. So, if you've recently gone through a terribly difficult breakup, such as the termination of a passionate long-term relationship, your Root Chakra might feel shattered because the sudden abandonment causes us to doubt our security and sense of belonging. This damage to our Root Chakra then promotes and promulgates feelings of anxiety, fear, and stress because this is all we have when we no longer feel secure with ourselves. In this scenario, you've been thrown off-balance, and if you do not rebalance your Root Chakra, soon then the rest of your Chakras will begin to respond. They'll attempt to restore balance, but because they cannot directly command the Root Chakra, they'll instead just respond by unbalancing themselves in the *opposite* direction.

So, when our Sacral Chakra goes into overdrive to make up for the now underactive or blocked Root, we experience heightened emotion. We begin to find ourselves attaching quickly to others, often while overstepping some boundaries, all the while being subjected to terrible mood swings because underlying all this is still our fear of abandonment brought about by our damaged Root. If you've ever been in a situation where you found yourself getting re-attached to someone new much faster than normal, even if your new attachment was one-sided, then perhaps this example offers an explanation for the decisions you made during the turmoil you were in. Complicating the matter, of course, is that in reality it's not just your Root that'd be hurt, but often your Heart Chakra, too.

For the sake of keeping the example simple, we won't factor that aspect in, but hopefully being aware of it illustrates just how tangled and off-balance our Chakras can get when we undergo great emotional strain. Even something as simple as moving houses or changing schools can disrupt your Root Chakra if it wasn't your choice to leave, especially if you struggle to find familiar faces in your new environment.

What it Means to be In Balance

However, in order to understand whether we are unbalanced or not, it pays to have perspective. What does "balance" feel like? It can take a lot of effort to achieve balance, but once balance has been achieved, the result is that your Chakras can now spin effortlessly, passing energy both in and out appropriately according to your environment. When our Chakras are all in harmony, we feel alive. We begin to see the beauty in life, and our acknowledgement of that beauty is not shattered with the introduction of inconvenience or tragedy. When we are in balance, we are able to see pain without being overcome and debilitated by it. We are able to love another person without feeling perpetually hungry for them.

We are able to have conversations we enjoy without feeling like we're forcing them on others, and without feeling as if we're the ones expending all the energy and making all the effort to make them happen. We speak freely, and feel full. We instinctively realize who we can be honest with, and passively broaden that list by gaining a better understanding of how best to express the truth, without embellishment or smoke and mirrors. We are also able to listen to the perspectives of others. We are able to hear criticism without taking it personally, and are able to recognize the grains of truth in another's words even if we do not believe everything that they're saying.

We'll also have a better understanding of what really matters to a person when they speak, and what they're just exaggerating in a desperate attempt to have their voice finally be heard. And, therefore, you'll finally hear.

If the seven main Chakras form as a collective to become a great river, then being in balance is like having a river that is completely undammed and undiverted. Through no active effort on your part, it flows, and it naturally helps bring life to all around it. Life comes to it voluntarily, knowing it will find refreshment at its banks. When you have such a river, you do not fear who will stay or go, for you'll intuitively know where those in your life stand in relation to you and how to connect with them. If you realize they might want to leave, you won't begrudge them for it because you'll know you've done all you can, and that goodbyes aren't necessarily forever.

Being balanced is also about enjoying the present, because realistically our balance is never permanent and, ironically, stressing too much about staying in balance in the future can upset our balance itself. When we are balanced, then, we appreciate what we have with us in this moment right now. Although the wise will still prepare for the future, it won't be at the expense of our appreciation for our present.

How to Achieve Balance

Now, while it is true that one unbalanced Chakra can cause the rest to go a little haywire, it is also true that taking the time to balance or reseat even one can help bring peace to the other six. For most individuals, the majority of their Chakras are actually already dormant or blocked in some manner, while others tend to be massively overworked. In extreme cases, you might even feel like part of you has "burned out." The good news is that Chakras do not die, and no damage they sustain is irreversible. They are all energy, all reflections of you and how your mind and body interconnect. As long as you can breathe, you can heal your Chakras.

To heal them is thankfully a very simple procedure. There is no medication or surgery required, simply meditation. In the same way that exercise can help with hormone regulation, proper meditation can aid you in regulating and re-aligning each of your Chakras. Meditation is best accompanied with visualizing the color of the Chakra you wish to focus on, as well as repeating its mantras and syllables. Additional Chakra healing methods will be covered in Chapters 9-10, and more everyday balancing methods will be covered chapter by chapter.

To start you off, however, you can follow this basic meditation technique: first, you'll need to find a place of relative peace. This is usually your bedroom or sitting room. However, any space will do if you can be completely certain that you'll be safe and undisturbed if you zone out for thirty minutes. Then, seat yourself comfortably on the floor. If the floor is too hard, you can use something soft to cushion your rear against the ground. Make sure your legs are crossed in front of you when you sit, then hold your spine upright, but not strained. Let your hands rest and relax on top of your knees. Then, begin to breathe deeply and evenly. This is basic meditation that will clear your mind. Should thirty minutes seem too daunting, aim for ten and gradually grow from there. Practice this, and you'll lay the foundation needed for you to clear your Chakras.

Which Chakra Do I Start With?

If you're a complete beginner, I highly recommend learning about and meditating on each Chakra in the order presented in this book to awaken them, which is a priming process for healing and balancing. Once you've read this book in its entirety, you will then be ready to skip around as you see fit according to the questionnaire in Chapter 9 as well as your own common sense.

Ancient Vedic belief taught that our energy flows from our Root to our Crown, and that therefore you'd get the best results if you removed blockages "upstream" by your Root before attempting to undam your flow lower down.

If this sounds familiar to you at all, it may be because of similarities this Vedic thought shares with Maslow's Hierarchy of Needs, a popular psychology theory that's often used and cited by students in Business. Just as Maslow's needs flowed from the most basic (food, shelter) to the highest and most cerebral (active self-improvement and creation, the most divine of expressions), so too do our Chakras flow from the most basic physical needs to the loftiest spiritual goals.

Where the ancient Chakra model surpasses Maslow's, however, is that the Root is only one of seven energy circles within us, and yet it accounts for three of the five stages in Maslow's pyramid (shelter, safety *and* belonging). This shows that the ancients were not only onto something, but have already explored the matter in great depth, especially since they found methods of ameliorating or slaking these needs without needing to acquire additional resources. Unlike Maslow's model, which focuses on acquisition to meet needs, the examination of Chakras usually allows you to meet needs by addressing what you already have. To begin with your Root, continue to the next chapter.

Chapter 2:

Your Root

Now, you already know a little bit about the Root thanks to our earlier examples, but let's dig a little deeper.

Your Root Chakra is one of your Chakras of Matter. In Sanskrit, it is called *Mūlādhāra,* which is commonly translated as "root support" but can also be understood as "foundation of origin" or "basis for essence." It is the energy manifestation of one of the most basic affirmations in life; that we belong in this world, and that it'll provide what we need to survive. Understanding this basic concept on an instinctual level is what provides us with a will to live and overcome challenges, and this Chakra is what provides us with this instinctual understanding. This means it not only governs your need for safety and shelter, but also for resources. It also deals with the need for emotional attachment at its most instinctive level. It does not, however, deal with conscious strategies for acquisition, nor is it responsible for higher forms of love on its own; it merely enables them through subconsciously reminding you that you're allowed to take up space, and that claiming resources or being in relationships is a thing you can do.

Feeling secure in our position, believing we are needed or have purpose, and feeling comfortable that we can procure what we need to operate at a basic level are all vital cornerstones in the foundation needed to engage in higher pursuits. This is one of the reasons we call this Chakra the "Root." The other reason is that this Chakra exists within us before we are even born. It exists in the base of our spine before it is even fully formed. Thus, we can also understand it as the "Root" Chakra in the sense that it has been with us from the very beginning of life, before those who would love us might even have declared us alive.

Colors and Symbols

When you wish to meditate on your Root, envision first the color red. Red is this Chakra's color, and its symbols are the Square, the Earth, and the Four-Petaled Lotus. Do not overthink this, as these names are exactly what they describe. A Square is a square, for instance. So if you know what a square looks like, envisioning a red one can help you meditate on your Root, and likewise for earth/soil/solid matter or a four-petaled lotus. Envisioning a red four-petaled lotus with a square within its center tends to be the most effective, and many who take interest in Chakras will draw their lotus in a stylized fashion that allows them to incorporate the square into its design. This process is followed similarly by later Chakras, as you'll see, but I digress.

To enhance your connection to your Root while meditating, get into a habit of reciting its mantra between breaths: "Lam," or "Lang." Affirmations you can state to aid in meditating on your Root can include, "I have a right to be here. Like the tree on the ground or the star in the sky, I have a right to be here," or, "In this moment, I am connected to my body. In this moment, I am safe. In this moment, I am secure."

Is Your Root Off-Balance?

As our Root Chakra is with us from such an early period in our lives, it should come as no surprise to hear that our childhood experiences can often hold a huge impact on how naturally balanced our Root tends to be. Remember, your Root is the manifestation of your will to live, and your belief that your needs for survival, safety, and belonging will be met. As a child, how were these ideas affirmed within you? Were they able to be consistent in how they provided food, water, shelter, and love? Or were things chaotic, constantly changing, or uncertain?

Most of us have had to deal with some degree of uncertainty growing up, and how we handled it forms a huge part of what makes our Root Chakra what it is today. When you are completely powerless in a situation, however, such as when you're still an infant, having delays or inconsistencies in your basic needs being provided could mean that your Root Chakra remains blocked to this day.

Growing up, other events that could've shaken your Root off-balance include things such as moving houses, divorce, unemployment, heavy break-ups (as described before), and similar situations where you must constantly change and shift your means in order to continue finding sustenance, whether physical or emotional. Any form of rejection or betrayal can shake your Root Chakra if it directly impacts your ability to maintain your standards of living or if it makes you question your right to exist. This link with instinctual self-worth can mean that if you've ever been forced to violate a deeply-held principle or ever catastrophically failed at something you usually take pride in, your Root has likely been shaken during these events, too.

However, being off-balance isn't something that is caused just by loss or hurt. Balance can also be upset by an overfed Chakra. For instance, what if your family provided you not only with what you needed on a consistent basis, but with significantly more than you needed on a consistent basis? What if you were spoiled? Becoming dependent on luxuries can also be a threat to your Root, as all it'd take to unbalance it is the deprivation of the luxury. While it is true that an inactive Root can lead to psychological issues, an overfed Root is far more easily bruised.

Symptoms of an Off-Balance Root

Of course, despite all you have been through, it's possible that your Root may be fine. If you're still unsure whether or not your Root needs attention, ask yourself the following questions.

Do you have an eating disorder? This can be a touchy topic, as many of us connect how we eat to our self-image, but it's important to answer yourself honestly. Do you eat more than you need to survive? Are you eating so little that you're constantly feeling tired or wasting away? If so, why? No one eats perfectly all the time, so don't overthink this or be too hard on yourself. Strange eating habits alone don't necessarily mean an upset Root. That said, the more severe your eating disorder, the more likely it is that your Root Chakra needs attention.

How cynical are you? Building on that, how likely are you to take more than you need when presented with the opportunity?

A balanced Root affirms your right to exist, and assures you that you are able to find a way to the resources needed to live when you need them. When our Root is dormant or failing, however, we automatically take on more pessimistic or selfish mindsets because we no longer believe the world will provide for us and reward our efforts in a reliable manner. When our Root is dormant, our behavior drives us to take more for ourselves when we have the opportunity, because we fear we won't have the opportunity again the next time we need it. This links back to infant development, and how consistently your basic needs were met during your formative years. It can also link back to more recent experiences, like a retrenchment or failed job interview. Our Root tends to shrink when dealing with the more negative emotions associated with our "survival mode."

Speaking of survival mode, do you find yourself constantly making decisions out of fear? Write down a list of your most personal values - between five and ten is fine. If something like "security" or "safety" is ranking among your highest, it could be a sign that your Root is off-balance. Of course, we always want to be safe. However, if you consciously choose to rank safety so highly, it might be because you do not currently *feel* safe, which is a classic sign of a dormant Root.

Take a moment to reflect on your actions. If the majority of your choices have been made for the sake of trying to guarantee your own safety and security (or maybe the security of those closest to you, like your child), or if you find your decision-making process is ruled firstly by fear, then you certainly have an upset Root.

Linking to this, those who have chronic anxiety or frequent panic attacks are almost certainly long-term sufferers of a dormant or shrunken Root.

Why Healing Your Root Is Important

Now, a lot of the symptoms of an imbalanced Root might not sound like a bad thing if you're living in a desperate situation. In fact, they might even sound like the reasonable thing to be. In these scenarios, why is it important then that we keep our Root in balance?

First, when we keep making decisions only through fear, we'll soon forego trying to reach out and take advantage of what's around us. For instance, maybe you won't take advantage of a new shop or service nearby because you aren't familiar with the area, and are afraid you'll get lost or hurt. Maybe you'll eventually stop trying to get interviews because you fear you'll just be rejected again and waste your time. Or maybe you'll even consider taking your own life, out of the fear that even if you do make it through everything, nobody will care and you'll never have a place where you feel like you'll belong. The longer our Root lies damaged, the more we'll begin to doubt things we used to feel we could count on. The less we feel we can count on what we have, the harder it is to make plans due to the amount of unknown variables we now have. The harder it is to make plans, the fewer effective decisions we're able to make. Eventually, one devolves from making decisions through fear to being *paralyzed* by fear. Aptly, the physical manifestations of a poor Root are constant exhaustion as well as pain in the legs and spine, likely caused by a combination of poor eating and high stress.

In contrast, our Root is what keeps us calm and, well, *rooted* in reality by reminding us that we're still alive, that we aren't out of the race yet, and that there's still the possibility of laying a firm foundation amidst our changing circumstances. Change doesn't always mean things get worse; given time, it allows situations to improve, too.

Now, it's natural to be afraid, unsure, or opportunistic from time to time. But we cannot constantly sit and stew in that state of being for too long, otherwise we just become less certain, less capable, and more frantic.

Helping your Root stay balanced will help you retain your will to live, as well as retain your instinctive sense of purpose in survival. It also reminds us that it is possible to have known values in life, and it helps us build trust wisely in values that can be known. There might still be fear, but there'll also be hope, and this will drive you to keep doing whatever needs to be done to get by. Your Root is what allows you to continue taking value in your own life, and therefore continue to fight for both its sustenance and dignity. If your Root is allowed to die, you become wholly dependent on others again with little will or drive of your own, and this state of being only works if these are the kind of people who are willing and able to help you build your Root back up.

Open Your Root

To open your Root and take care of it are extremely easy even if we ignore the meditation technique described earlier.

For instance, stand up for yourself. In this instance, the meaning is literal; stand upright, place your feet shoulder-width apart from one another, and let your arms, head, and torso relax. When we're living in stress and fear all the time, it's not unusual that we begin to subconsciously tense up. So now, make the conscious decision to let your muscles relax. They aren't doing anything right now and could frankly do with a break. Next, let your hips sway forward very gently. Feel your pelvis push forward a bit, as if to discreetly brush against a lover's lower-body when you embrace, but not so far that you begin to lose balance. Now, envision roots growing from your toes into the ground. Begin to breathe deeply, in and out. With every exhalation, feel your roots penetrating more deeply, drawing more energy up to you.

This is for if your Root imbalance is making you feel constantly insecure. If you're feeling more pessimistic, however, it may be better to try this: exert active power over the small things you can control. Apply this not to people, however, only things. At its most basic, this means performing household chores. If you're feeling grubby, go take a shower and scrub the dirt off. If your room is looking a little dinky or cramped, do what you can to tidy it, organize it, let go of what you don't need and rediscover what you do. While doing this, it is important that you maintain consciousness of every single move you make. Do not let your mind wander away; keep it in the present, and keep it focused on your muscles and how they expand and contract on demand to help you accomplish basic domestic tasks.

In the case of showering, be aware of the sensation of water against your skin. Is it sharp and icy? Is it warm and reassuring? How does the soap feel against it? Smooth, soft, and slippery? Or maybe it is more coarse, but leaves you feeling sensitive and fresh. Mindfulness is vital when you attempt to open and balance your Root.

But what if your muscles ache too much, or you've already washed yourself and feel another scrub today might be a waste? Then you can open your Root through dancing and stretching instead. Very gently, move your muscles around. Slide your shoulder blades up and down your back. Stretch your arms wide above your head, like a cartoon character getting out of bed. Try to balance on the very tips of your toes, and feel your body as muscle and bone begins to click back into place according to your movements. You can create your own freeform dance made up of nothing but stretches that you find soothing or comfortable. Wave your hands in the air firmly, but gently. Kick your legs out. Pretend you're fencing. Anything that scrapes the metaphorical rust off your joints will help you open up your Root.

If that sounds too crazy for you, then a gentler way of helping is by performing a yoga pose called the "Downward-Facing Dog," which can be performed by anyone who isn't late into their pregnancy. If you aren't pregnant, but have headaches or high blood pressure, make sure you have something to support the weight of your head throughout this stretch.

Now, to perform it, go down onto the floor on your hands and knees. Again, use a cushion if it helps. Align your knees with your hips and place your hands slightly forward from the line of your shoulders. Make sure your hands spread their fingers out, with the index fingers ideally being parallel. Also ensure that the bases of your toes are in contact with the floor.

Now, using your hands and toes to support yourself, lift your knees away from the ground. At this point, ensure that your knees are still bent, and that the heels of your feet haven't made contact with the ground yet. Try stretching your tailbone away from your pelvis and towards the ceiling, though take care not to go too far. You might feel a little burn, but if it's hurting, stop and take it back a notch.

When you're ready, take a breath and, as you exhale, push your thighs further up so that you're now resting on both your hands and the soles of your feet. At this point, your knees can be straight, but not so straight that you cannot push them back further; do not lock your joints. Let the front of your pelvis narrow, then make your shoulder blades taut against your back before widening them and lowering them towards your tailbone. While this is happening, your hands should be actively supporting your weight. Be sure to keep your head up between your shoulders or upper arms too. It shouldn't hang.

After three minutes in this pose, relax.

Further Lifestyle Changes to Open Your Root

Helping your Root stay active on a daily basis doesn't have to mean stretches, dances, and chores. Adopting a high-protein, high vitamin C diet with root vegetables (excuse the pun) can work wonders for helping your body realign a confused Root. Excellent foods tend to be strawberries, cherries, and tomatoes, along with spinach, almonds, beans, beets, garlic, and potatoes; root vegetables of all kinds are especially good due to their connection with the Earth. The act of cooking is also a great way to help soothe your Root, so it is better if you prepare these meals yourself rather than delegating the task to a family member or ordering takeout. If you don't take yourself for a good cook, don't worry; just keep your meals simple, read online recipes carefully, and avoid working with meats until you're more sure of yourself. You'll soon find great peace in creating sustenance that you can then enjoy, and doing so consistently helps make you the master of your own Root.

Other activities that can aid in reawakening your Root include working with the Earth. This could mean toiling as a gardener or it could mean visiting the beach to build a sand castle.

It could also mean going for a hike on a fresh and secure trail. Such a walk among nature will allow you to reconnect with the idea of Earth without having to contend with the dangers normally associated with the wild. Being among nature, seeing its beauty and plenty, without feeling under threat will work wonders for the state of your Root.

In the long term, your Root will be happiest if you deeply familiarize yourself with a few places no matter what they are, so that you know their terrain inside and out, feeling completely safe within them. The more places you familiarize yourself with, the further you'll be able to travel without upsetting your Root.

Chapter 3:

Your Sacral Chakra

The next Chakra of Matter, your Sacral Chakra, is known in Sanskrit as the *Svadhisthana*, which can be translated as "the place where the self lives." A healthy Sacral Chakra is the foundation of a self-aware and supportive ego. While it can be quite close to your Root in terms of energy, it has its own unique nuances and other factors to be aware of.

For instance, while your Root deals with family on an instinctual and familiar level, especially for the purposes of meeting basic needs, your Sacral Chakra is geared more towards helping you explore and develop relationships outside of that, as well as help you take existing relationships to the next level.

While your Root is invested first and foremost in your will and right to survive and thrive, your Sacral Chakra cares more about your relationships directly. It is also what gives you courage to step away from the status quo to help you define and pursue your survival independently, defining it on your own terms. Your Sacral Chakra prevents your Root from entrapping you or making you brittle. In fact, out of all your Chakras, your Sacral one places the heaviest focus on creativity and passion, and this passionate energy flows through all that you enjoy whether it be your work, your favorite pastime, a cherished romance, or even a session of lovemaking.

Similarly to your Root, a balanced Sacral will help you overcome fear, and solidify your identity in relation to the rest of the world. It also plays a heavy role in how you interact with temptations that you come across in day-to-day life, things that aren't necessary for your physical survival, feeling of safety, or general well-being, but still hold some sway over you due to your chemistry with the subject matter.

Finally, where the Root is focused heavily on what you can take from the world to fulfill yourself, your Sacral Chakra is more concerned in showing you what you can *give* to fulfill yourself. This is partially why it is regarded as our creative energy center among the Chakras; whether you're giving the world a message, a beautiful new perspective, insight into the lives of others, or an orgasm, your ability to do so in a way that generates value and meaning while creating a sense of fulfillment within yourself is dependent on your ability to recognize and explore new and pleasurable ways of giving, ways that benefit not only the consumer, but also you, whether you're an artistic creator or a meticulous data compiler.

Colors and Symbols

When you wish to meditate on your Sacral Chakra, envision a wheel of orange light, this Chakra's color. Unlike the Root, which sits at the base of your spine, your Sacral Chakra sits about two inches below your belly button. While the Root is most often associated with our adrenal gland (due to the strong links to fear, perseverance, and survival), our Sacral is most often associated with our reproductive organs. If you're a woman, it's specifically associated with your womb due to its immense creative powers.

In terms of symbols, your Sacral Chakra is represented by a Six-Petaled Lotus, the shape of a Crescent Moon, and the element of Water, emphasizing its need to flow and change, and to try and explore new things. Although this might sound antagonistic to the familiarity-loving Root, note that all seven of your

Chakras can work in harmony. It is fully possible to satisfy both your Root and your Sacral by choosing to explore things outside of your comfort zone, just so long as you are not placing yourself in obvious or serious physical danger, or behaving irresponsibly with your resources. Trying new things within your means will allow you to keep both of these aspects of yourself in balance as you live your life.

To achieve the strongest and most focused connection with your Sacral Chakra during meditation, repeat affirmations to yourself such as, "What I offer the world is enough, and I love what I create for it," or, "I possess a vibrant body. I love it, and feel comfortable inside it. I know I can meet the change in my life and make the best of my future."

In general, focus on affirmations which reinforce that you have a right to create, to experiment, to try new things, to redefine dynamics in your life, and to feel comfortable within your physical form. In general, focus on where you can grow long-lasting joy. Its seed-syllable or mantra is "Vam." So, if you wanted to focus on your Root and Sacral Chakras simultaneously, you might repeat, "Lam-Vam, Lam-Vam, Lam-Vam." Note that the "a" sound in these syllables sounds like the "u" from "umpire" when spoken aloud, rather than the "a" from "apple."

Checking Your Sacral Chakra for Balance

Because our Sacral Chakra guides our creative energy, it must by virtue also hold sway over our playfulness and overall sense of humor. Playfulness fuels imagination, and a sense of humor allows us to look at things from unexpected angles, both of which are traits that any creative individual would find useful. The dependence of creativity on playfulness and humor is also why the Sacral Chakra is commonly attributed as the Chakra of Pleasure; it wants us to have fun and enjoy our undertakings.

But what if you do not feel creative? Most of us have surprisingly dormant Sacral Chakras. However, this is not because you are not creative, but rather because you may have been shaken too often in the past without realignment.

While our Root may be shaken by the termination of a long term, deeply-valued relationship or the removal of a vital resource from our environment, our Sacral Chakras by comparison tend to be shaken by less extreme, more common events.

For example, something as relatively light as being rejected by a crush or infatuation is enough to shake your Sacral Chakra. Even though you might barely know them, even though you do not have any relationship or exchange of value with them, their rejection is still enough to wobble your Sacral because it calls into question your ability to provide value to others. It might even make you question if you'll find someone to share your pleasures with.

Likewise, every time your creative output has been offended or denigrated, your Sacral has been wobbled. Whether it was a peer mocking your drawing ability in school, or an investor rejecting your business proposal through a feigned veneer of politeness, having a creative undertaking be rejected by another is sure to upset your Sacral.

However, it is possible to avoid these shakes in the future by taking yourself less seriously and by having a better sense of humor. Although you should always continue to value your creative potential as well as any output you choose to undertake, those with a balanced Sacral Chakra acknowledge that the world doesn't move at their pace. Although our Sacral helps define our ego, this also means creating realistic expectations of its limits.

This means one with a healthy Sacral will continue producing things creatively. If a project fails, they'll continue it until satisfaction or until they find a more worthy channel for their creative energy. They recognize that everyone has their own Chakras, their own needs that need filling, and although they have fun and enjoy creating things, they do not expect everyone to be able to resonate with everything they do all the time. No one is *that* good. This means if one has a healthy Sacral, they can avoid being thrown off-balance by rejection through sincerely understanding that the rejection wasn't personal, that usually it isn't someone saying your work is bad so much as they're saying they just don't need its energy right now.

This allows the individual with the healthy Sacral to start over and either create work with the correct energy for that person, or go out and seek new people who need the kind of energy their original work has (George Lucas did this several times as he searched for investors who'd resonate with *Star Wars*, for instance).

In contrast, because someone with an upset Sacral will be less playful and have a poor sense of humor, they will take all rejection or criticism personally. This consequently means they'll be offended more easily, as the ego will lose track of where it should be, and will start over-attributing things to itself. When the Sacral Chakra is imbalanced, instead of thinking, "What can I do to express my creativity to show value to those I care about?" your ego will instead think, "They hate me and what I do. They have no need for it, and I should give up," and yet, if you give up, you cut your potential off.

You must never give up. This doesn't mean stubbornly sticking with an idea until the bitter end, but it does mean always trying out new ideas, exploring your playful and creative side until there is harmony between your work and those you wish to share it with.

This is vital, because continuing to let your Sacral shrink can have other adverse effects. If you become too afraid to play and too afraid to step outside the box, then you may find yourself having trouble in bed; the mere thought of pleasurable sex with wrack you with guilt, tainting any excitement you might have with a fear and loathing that ruins your libido.

In a more general sense, you might have trouble even connecting to others at all, and feel as if you need to manipulate or coerce them to stay or work with you. You'll feel detached, neglecting your own true desires while simultaneously feeling unsure that you're truly meeting anyone else's.

As a result, your relationships will inherently become more abusive, because you'll constantly feel afraid that you're too dry, too boring, and unneeded by others. These feelings can be exacerbated if you also suffer from the physical symptoms of an imbalanced Sacral Chakra, such as infertility, impotency, and lower back and kidney pains. However, this does not need to be your reality, and the fear that you are objectively boring is objectively untrue. This world has a space for you, and you do not need to constantly exert power and compulsion to keep that space open.

Open Your Sacral Chakra

That said, you cannot depend on others to assert that affirmation for you. Not unless you're fine with placing all your creative power and inspiration in the hands and whims of others. No, what you have is far too precious to leave about so carelessly.

In everyday life, one of the best things you can do to realign your Sacral Chakra is engage in a diet of teas, soups, seeds, and fleshy fruits, particularly coconuts and oranges. These nourishing foods will help take the edge off any anxiety that may be blocking your creative flow. The next best thing you can do is visit the beach, or perhaps a nearby lake or stream. Sit on the sand or soil and let the sound of the waves wash over you.

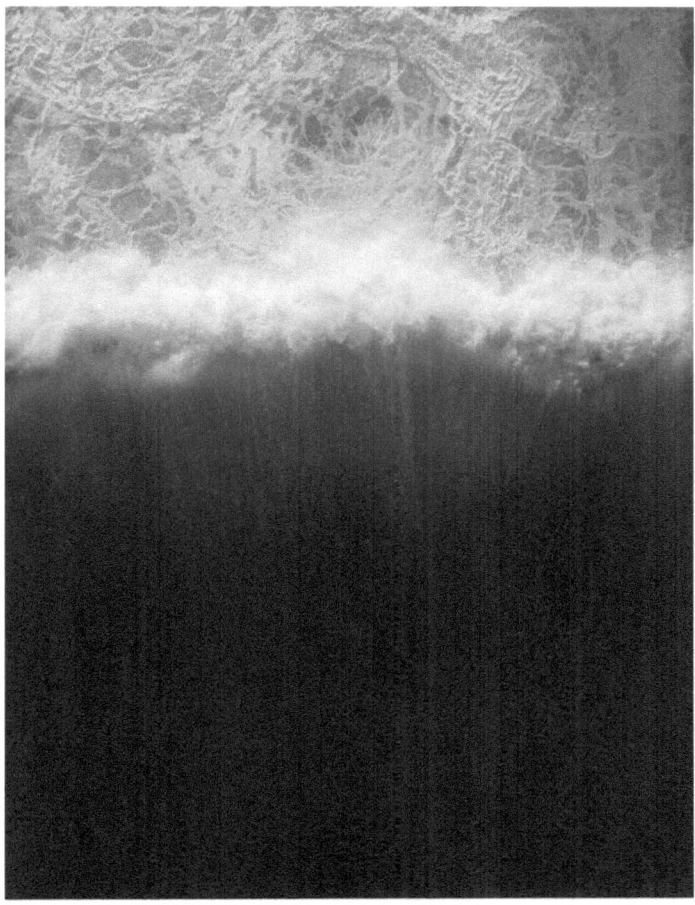

Even better is swimming. Spending time with the water will subtly remind you of the fluidity of life, a necessary awareness for the creative thinker. Observe how the shape of water changes as it ripples. Observe how it gleams under the sunlight, and how its color changes as clouds move over and darkness leaks into the sky. Dance next to the water. If you felt shy before about doing a crazy dance for your Root, at least perform one for your Sacral; aim to move so that your joints feel loose and free again; aim to help your muscles stretch and freshen out.

Keep a journal, so that when your stifled inspiration does break through and strike, you can immediately draw it or write about it. Don't worry about being Rembrandt or Shakespeare, just be you. Part of having a centered Sacral Chakra means being at peace with who you are, and living according to your own integrity rather than being subsumed by choosing to live in another's shadow.

Besides, with both experience and further Sacral alignment, you'll come to love your work for what it is, as will those around you if your creations are considerate of their needs. When you do vaguely feel like playing, do so. For fathers especially, one of the best things you can do is play a game of catch with your child. This not only helps assert the child's Root, but also the father's Sacral. Drawing, cooking, or painting together are also great if neither you nor the child are the sporty type. Make more time for the friends you have. If you do not have many friends, or they are not available, do not stress.

After all, being overly-attached or dependent on others is a symptom of an imbalanced Sacral, so you won't be rebalancing it by chasing after people when they're not around. Simply spend time with them when they can be around, but don't expect them to always be available. Appreciate what time you have; treat it as if it were precious jade.

When others cannot be around, remember that you still have yourself. Part of loving your creations stems from being able to love and acknowledge yourself. This helps your ego to relax and stop investing all its worth in external forces; loving your work is not the same as believing it to be perfect, nor is it the same as feeling personally offended when given suggestions on how to improve. Investing too heavily in external forces to keep your ego afloat means you might get too enraged or saddened by advice to take it to heart, or to properly consider it in the context of your objectives. Through this, you spoil your work as you might spoil a child.

So, show your inner child some meaningful affection instead by undertaking a hobby you enjoy. Pick something that you can do for yourself, first and foremost, allowing you to rebuild your creative energy to the point where you can confidently share it with others again. This could mean building model trains, or it could mean creating your own characters and even entire worlds through writing or penmanship. As difficult as it may be to drum up the inspiration to even engage in a hobby, realigning your Sacral and keeping it open requires you to be fearless in engaging with activities that you love.

The next way to help your Sacral Chakra realign is through empathy. Remember when we mentioned that people do not judge what we create based on who we are personally, but rather based on how what we've made resonates with their own needs and failings? While a healthy ego will recognize that it is not perfect, a Sacral Chakra that wishes to be healthy too will recognize that *no one* is perfect, nor will it expect them to be. Practicing thought exercises where you consider why a person may be acting a certain way, and considering when you yourself might act similarly, will help your creative energies flow again by virtue of taking advantage of multiple perspectives. This exercise is also a form of creative play.

Finally, because your Sacral Chakra is linked with sensuality and desire, you can coax it out through aromatherapy. The best essential oils for this purpose tend to be rose, sandalwood, cardamom, and orange.

These all give off scents that appeal to the physical senses, helping the body ease into a soft mood and relax a tad, which can be just the starting point a Sacral realignment needs.

To amplify this effect, consider keeping moonstones or especially carnelians with you, which are known to stimulate the Sacral Chakra. These beautiful gemstones also have the added benefit of being a fun and exciting challenge to draw, as well as potentially inspire poetry, metaphors and the like. Their cool and smooth surface against your hand will further help you stay conscious of your skin, making it easier to step back inside your body and continue your Sacral reawakening.

Chapter 4:

Your Solar Plexus

This is your third Chakra of Matter. In Sanskrit, your Solar Plexus Chakra is known as *Manipura*, which translates roughly into "lustrous jewel," "shining crystal," or "city/throne of gems," and it can be found between your belly button and your sternum. In English, we call it the "Solar Plexus" due to it lining up almost perfectly with the cluster of nerve fibers of the same name. While your Root is your energy manifestation of your right to live, and your Sacral Chakra is your right to create and enjoy, your Solar Plexus is expressly your right to be an individual, and your right to assert your will within your life.

If your Sacral Chakra is the dawn of your ego, your Solar Plexus is its core and culmination, at least as far as Matter is concerned. It balances your previous two Chakras through tempering your will to live and your desire to experience and create. This is achieved by introducing, reinforcing, and supporting concepts of self-discipline, self-reliance, and self-mastery.

This is the Chakra that prevents your Sacral from devolving into perversion or hedonism. This is the Chakra that raises you above and beyond the need to survive. This is the Chakra that begins to distinguish your soul from that of the common animal. Without your Solar Plexus, your Sacral Chakra would struggle to keep you authentic to yourself, and you'd become lost, defined by nothing but the drive to find new experiences, new sensations. Your Sacral Chakra lets you play and create, but without the support of your Solar Plexus it won't stick with you once you start struggling or feeling bored. Without your Solar Plexus, your Sacral Chakra wouldn't be able to fully realize any of its grand dreams and desires in a complete and practical form.

Likewise, without your Solar Plexus, your Root would struggle to give you direction beyond what to eat, who to trust, and where to sleep. It'd imbue you with the innate sense of purpose needed for self-preservation, but beyond that wouldn't be able to show or direct your immense potential. Without your Solar Plexus, you wouldn't have the drive to stand up for beliefs, ideals, or anything bigger than you for that matter, nor would you have the confidence to follow through on any plan or strategy outside of what your Root deems absolutely necessary. This applies even more so if the activity in question doesn't carry the creative and pleasurable connotations that tends to sway the Sacral.

Your Solar Plexus, then, is what allows you to find purpose and express intention above and beyond basic needs or simple pleasures, and it forms the foundation for higher thinking and expanded emotional awareness. Whereas the previous two Chakras ask only how you can fulfill yourself, both through giving and through receiving, your Solar Plexus instead asks how you can *define* yourself. Who are you? What do you wish to accomplish while you're here? If there are multiple paths to a goal, which one are you more likely to take? What would you be willing to sacrifice first, and what would you protect to your dying breath?

When you create, what do you create? Why? There are so many ways to survive, so many ways to create pleasure, so why choose the way you are choosing now? Are you sure it is the best way that you can follow right now?

Your Solar Plexus gives you an innate understanding of these questions, thereby empowering you with the self-confidence needed to carry out your decisions and propel yourself through life according to what matters most to you. Through your Solar Plexus, your needs and desires can be solidly unified under long-term goals of your choice, allowing the accomplishment of great and unique deeds through the cooperation amongst your energies.

Colors and Symbols

When meditating on your Solar Plexus, envision Yellow, which is its color. You may begin to notice that your Chakras will form a rainbow of energy when they're all in alignment. This is no coincidence. Just as every color in the rainbow makes up the spectrum of visible light, so does the energy of each Chakra make up the spectrum of celestial energy that can manifest through your mortal form. They are not aspects in isolation, but rather parts of a greater whole that we can choose to focus on selectively.

In terms of symbols, your Solar Plexus is best represented through the Ten-Petaled Lotus, through an upside-down equilateral Triangle, and through the element of Fire, which represents the sheer light and warmth with which a healthy and fully-realized personality can shine. When meditating, it is invoked with the mantra seed-syllable "Ram," which as before is best repeated while imagining a yellow ten-petaled lotus with the symbolic shape in its center.

Affirmations that can aid in the meditative process include phrases such as, "I can feel my power. I can acknowledge that I am always free to choose. I can always make the choice to direct my own life. I can trust my intuition, my inner voice. I can follow it whenever it speaks to me. I can thank it when it helps me succeed, and I can forgive it if it leads me astray."

The Importance of Balance in the Solar Plexus

Your Solar Plexus is what keeps you confident and motivated. It is what imbues you with a feeling of responsibility. It is what allows you to trust in your own decision-making and advice. It is what allows you to trust yourself, and prevents you from balking when arriving at a crossroads. It is what allows you to overcome stagnation. Compare your Solar Plexus to a writer's outline, or an organization's core strategies or modus operandi. The outline is what gives the writer a maintained sense of motivation as they work, preventing them from being spun out of control the moment their inspiration fades. Likewise, the business strategy is what allows a company to keep making decisions that'll richly reward it in the long term, even if in the short-term it might mean making some sacrifices that seem to threaten its survival.

In both cases, strategies and outlines are what let us quickly make decisions in moments of doubt, as well as give us a foundation to return to when we encounter a dilemma that is holding us back. Our Solar Plexus acts much like an outline or a strategy, but on a more personal or instinctive level.

It is strengthened every time you accomplish something on your own merit, and is harmed every time you doubt or criticize yourself.

Of course, no one is perfect; we've all done things worthy of criticism, and sometimes our self-doubt is not without cause; to have no self-doubt at all is to believe you're infallible, which is tremendously arrogant.

What a truly peaceful and balanced Solar Plexus comes down to, then, is moderation. To determine which way we should moderate (become sterner with yourself or gentler on yourself), take a moment to examine the life you've experienced so far.

If you were constantly spoiled and praised, yet never acted on your own steam, then it might be that you have a powerful Sacral Chakra but a withered Solar Plexus. This is fairly easy to deal with, however. Other than putting more effort into giving yourself direction, you simply need to consider the advice under the next subheading.

But what if your parents were harsh and strict? Authoritarian parents can be helpful when it comes to giving us an overarching goal, but a common downfall in such a parenting method is that the child often isn't taught to fend for themselves or design life-affecting personal strategies independently. Parents who are too strict or controlling inadvertently teach their child to always defer to others for important decisions, thus making it difficult for them to deliberately carry out work or growth-related objectives outside of what they have express permission to do.

Those who endured such strict upbringing might therefore have quite a damaged Solar Plexus.

This is because a full, balanced flow of Chakral energy mandates us to occasionally be *proactive*—to make decisions, innovate solutions, or resolve problems through independent thought or critical thinking. Authoritarian parenting, in contrast, encourages children to be *reactive* instead — to make decisions that are overly-dependent upon parameters set and defined by external entities. The psychological effects, in the long term, can be quite similar to that of bullying (namely, a massive decline in the victim's self-esteem or ability to recognize and employ personal power), only more insidious and harder to escape due to the relationship dynamic between parent and child.

In childhood, this might have meant feeling constantly stressed out or unexpectedly releasing very rare yet devastating emotional outbursts, particularly outbursts of anger, judgement, stubbornness, or scathing criticism, all of which are signs of an unbalanced Solar Plexus. In adult life, this continues, but without your parents to look out for you anymore it'll mean you'll be like wet clay to the first thing you form an attachment with that you perceive to be greater or more authoritative than yourself, whether it is your boss, an expert, an official or, in tragic cases, your romantic partner.

This is what leads to us become people-pleasers. When we're encouraged not to believe in ourselves (when our Solar Plexus is thrown off-balance), we begin to make mistakes very similar to the one regarding criticism in Chapter 3; we begin to invest far too much of our self-worth in the perceptions of others. While a balanced Solar Plexus lets us define ourselves, and build ourselves around a solid and reliable constant, an off-balance Solar Plexus leaves us open to feeling defined by external forces that we can never truly control.

This is an even deeper calamity because no one can ever know you as well as you can know yourself. This means letting yourself be defined by someone else will *always* end up with you selling yourself short. This doesn't mean the opinions or perceptions of others aren't valid, of course, it just means that what a person sees in you is only a small fragment of a greater whole. Your character is like an iceberg; when you let others define you completely, while discounting your own thoughts and beliefs, then you'll never feel bigger than your tip.

When your Solar Plexus is balanced, however, the validation and confirmation of others no longer feels like a need; you will not place favor and disgrace alongside food and water. When your Solar Plexus is balanced, you'll not only feel comfortable exerting your will, but you'll feel comfortable doing so with minimum force, going along the path of least resistance to achieve your goals while playing to your strengths. Because you are the one setting parameters for your goals and behavior, you'll have an easier time matching your strengths to where they need to be, too. For instance, a man with over a decade of experience working in IT wouldn't be happy working as an accountant or design consultant, for instance, and if he has a balanced Solar Plexus he'll assertively request transfer into a department where his talents can be best employed.

In contrast, if this same man had a weak Solar Plexus, he'd likely feel victimized and mistreated in his position as a designer, and would feel powerless to change his situation despite the clear advantages in attempting to do so far outweighing any potential risks. He might even begin to hate his managers because of this, even though it really isn't their fault that he didn't speak up.

Opening Your Solar Plexus

While being reactive is a sign of an imbalanced Solar Plexus, this doesn't mean being inactive is the answer. While being reactive is a sign of blockage, inactivity, or indecisiveness, is a sign of near total dormancy. This doesn't mean you now have to take an active role in every opportunity or activity you're aware of, but it does mean balancing out strategic non-action with deliberate and intentional action.

Something to be aware of is that while a balanced Solar Plexus will award a feeling of power, that feeling of power alone is only one aspect of it; if you are still so caught up in the perceptions of others that you feel the need to use your power to manipulate them or plaster your own ideas over them, drowning them out for fear of what they might say, then your Solar Plexus is still out of balance. If you become overly harsh and critical towards others to break them down so that they will not even dare try to retaliate or question you, then your Solar Plexus is still out of balance; worse, you're likely unbalancing theirs, too.

When one behaves this way, it is often because one fears that the validation we've invested in ourselves is a lie, and that when confronted by the negative opinions of others our self-esteem will crumble. This does not lead to a balanced Solar Plexus.

To help unblock and balance this Chakra, practice admiring the power of others, but do not covet it, nor let your heart be cowed by it. Instead, choose to learn from it. Likewise, think before you speak, but do not hold your tongue out of fear of what might be said back.

Yearn to hear from others. Yearn to learn from them. Invest confidence in yourself; not confidence in that you are correct per se, but rather that there's potential value in your words if you are right, while at the same time recognizing that there often is no harm in being wrong. Define yourself not by your failures, but rather by the accomplishments those failures help you achieve. You cannot be great without learning, and you cannot learn without being willing to make a few mistakes.

If you wish to boost your confidence and assertiveness, or wish to help soften your aggressiveness and harshness, consider taking up a diet of corn, bananas, grain, potatoes, and herbal teas.

Add yellow into your wardrobe; it is a bright and cheerful color that pops beautifully against reds, blues, violets, blacks, and more. The best yellow would be a warm one, rather than cool or blue-tinted. In your day-to-day life, practice making personal decisions without consulting with others. Although not every decision will be perfect, you're still likely to enjoy the success rates you did previously while *learning things for yourself*. This will impart you with experience and personal power; the building blocks of self-reliance and a balanced Solar Plexus. These are building blocks you'd never earn if everyone always decided things for you.

When in a team environment, however, you will need to consult with others in order to operate effectively. Because decisions that directly affect an entire team or organization aren't *personal* decisions, the best way for you to keep your Solar Plexus open in these cases is through taking the initiative and speaking your mind. Communicate the ideas or thoughts that spark within you without apology or without doubting yourself; in a team dynamic, everyone else will want to question you, but not because they don't believe in you. They're questioning you to make sure you believe in yourself.

Their doubts are not an attack, but rather the start of a conversation. Rather than replying defensively, seek to reassure them through addressing their fears with your reasoning as well as making amendments when they correctly spot gaps. Remember, your character is an iceberg. Give them a taste of what's beneath the surface, and ideas that only sounded good in your head will begin to sound better and better coming out of your mouth.

Chapter 5:

Your Very Heart

This is your bridge between your Chakras of Matter and your Chakras of Energy. Although your physical heart beats constantly, your heart Chakra was first recorded in Sanskrit as *Anahata*, which means "Unbeaten." The implication is that no matter what hurts you've endured, no matter what battles or wars you've survived, your Heart Chakra never surrendered, even when the rest of you felt like it might have. It also implies forgiveness, to accept that once a wound has healed, it can be let go and that once you get back off the ground, you can choose to live and treat others as though you were never beaten.

Your Heart, then, is part of what lets you see people for what they are, and treat them according to who they are in the present, rather than who they are associated with, what they might do in the future, or what they have done in the past.

In terms of location, your Heart Chakra can be found just above your physical heart, meaning that unlike the rest of your Chakras it is not perfectly centered, but stands a little bit off to the left. Despite this, it is what holds you together. Even when it is off-balance, it plays a vital role in helping you heal and care for the rest of your Chakras. Through this Chakra, you can care for yourself, and you can care for others from a position of gratitude and strength, rather than exhaustion and simmering resentment. If your Sacral Chakra is what helps you give to others, adding value and forming connections for the sake of your self-validation and fulfillment, then your Heart Chakra is what enables you to do these same things *unconditionally,* which makes it easier for you to continue being kind and gentle toward others even when it does not directly benefit you.

Beyond this, your Heart Chakra endeavors to support and protect all other aspects of you as a person. For instance, it will help your Solar Plexus draw boundaries that prevent others from taking advantage of you. It'll help teach your Root who and what to trust, and helps your Sacral Chakra gain a deeper understanding of the energy and impulses it is supposed to master and direct. Ultimately, when we are in balance we *love* life, we *love* having fun, we *love* creating and experiencing pleasure, and we *love* being who we are.

Without a healthy sense of both self-love and a love for others, then, long-term balancing of your Chakras of Matter would not be possible. This is why we can say the Heart Chakra supports and protects.

Colors and Symbols of the Heart

When you wish to connect to your Heart through meditation, be sure to place extra focus on the awareness of your breath. Do not try to control it, just be aware. Feel how your body changes as oxygen flows through you, and feel how that flow changes in response to your thoughts and emotions compared to how it flows when you are at rest, or at peace. This is because the element of your Heart is Air. All life on this planet, whether on the Earth or in the Water, cannot live without Air. It is something we share with every heartbeat, every second of every day for as long as we're alive, and this sense of interconnectedness establishes your Heart as your first real step into expanding beyond yourself. Where the first three Chakras helped define yourself, your Heart helps you connect that self with all the other selves in the world.

The Heart Chakra's color is Green, and its other symbols are the Twelve-Petaled Lotus as well as the

Six-Pointed Star, which curiously bears a strong resemblance to the Star of David.

The Heart's mantra and seed-syllable is "Lam," phonetically pronounced "yaahm," and your mind's focus on this energy can be further strengthened through affirmations such as, "I have the right to choose, and the right to joy; therefore, I choose to be joyful in giving compassion and love," or, "I allow myself to be aware of my emotions, and endeavor to accept them for what they are no matter what form they take."

This doesn't mean acting out on your emotions, of course, but it does mean allowing you to feel them and come to terms with them. Ignoring a feeling does not make it go away, and can in fact lead to insidious deep-seated issues later down the line. Further helpful affirmations for bringing peace and balance to the Heart include, "I am open to love. I use my power of creation to create healthy, loving relationships that support me and those around me. When I do wrong and when I receive wrong, I open my heart to forgive others and to forgive myself."

Forgiveness does not mean pretending nothing ever happened, of course. Nor does it mean you don't have the right to respond to a wrong, or to try to correct it. Rather, forgiveness means you refuse to define yourself by your lowest moment, and likewise refuse to define others by theirs. You give both yourself and others room to grow and become better people, and you accept that no matter how much we improve, we'll never be perfect; therefore, we must always be ready to forgive.

Keeping Your Heart in Balance

It is quite rare that the Heart is shaken directly; more often than not, it unbalances only to make up for the hurts and pains of other Chakras. However, one of the pains most likely to reach up to your Heart is grief. Processing grief is your Heart's biggest challenge, and thus the emotion that is most likely to unbalance it. Paradoxically, those who wish to keep their Hearts in balance will not shut themselves away from that grief. They will let themselves feel it, completely and utterly. Not for even a moment will they consider showing anything less than how their hurt is making them feel.

This is because ignoring grief doesn't let us bypass it, merely postpone it and draw it out. This delay then leads to a lack of forgiveness. Going back to our Root-upsetting example, have you ever been in a situation where, after someone you deeply loved or cared for had seemingly abandoned you, you found it difficult to grow close to someone else after that?

On a subconscious level, you are comparing your new loved one to the one who hurt you, causing you to treat them more and more as if *they* were the one who hurt you. This is a sign that you have not yet forgiven, and have not yet chosen to fully resolve your grief. This is alright; grief is a deeply personal journey, and we must all go through it at our own pace, but then you need to be aware of how your grief might be making you feel, and how it might be causing you to treat others.

When our Hearts are off-balance, we feel numb. We tend to overreact to accidental slights from our loved ones, and even begin to judge ourselves with scathing inner remarks should our Solar Plexus be off-balance simultaneously.

As our Hearts are responsible for our sense of compassion and connection with others, when off-balance we see people less and less for what they are, and more and more for what we imagine them to be, especially if what we imagine fits into the self-pitying narrative we tend to develop while our Hearts are upset.

When we want to escape this and begin to re-open our Hearts to the world, it helps to put the shoe on the other foot. Rather than dwelling too heavily on how much a person has hurt you, or how harsh or unkind they have been, consider the harshness of life that they themselves may be quietly enduring. Believe it or not, most people on this planet are not harsh and vindictive on a daily basis, but how quickly do our tempers rise and hearts close when we bear terrible news, and how much more so when we feel as if we must bear it alone?

Maybe today you or someone you love was diagnosed with a terrible illness. Maybe last night you had a terrible sleep. Maybe you'd recently had a traumatic experience where a friend almost died. Maybe today you lost your job, or found out that the love of your life doesn't actually love you after all. Try as you might, the pain we experience from these events causes us to lash out at people who had nothing to do with it, and if we bury those feelings, trying to bottle them up, then we'll treat people poorly for it for years to come.

When others treat you poorly, then, take a moment to consider what they might have gone through. When you do this, you are preventing yourself from judging them too hastily, and giving yourself time to discern further context. You're also allowing yourself to experience empathy and try to connect to another human being; this is good for you as well as them, as all of these things help your Heart reawaken. Even if what you learn or experience leads you to draw up a boundary to protect yourself, this is fine. The aim is simply to avoid letting your pain, as well as the pain of others, diminish your own compassion; when you can be open with others, you can learn where best to position yourself in relation to them so that you can offer them maximum love without being dragged into the same dark place they're walking through.

But how do you know whether or not you're walking through a dark place yourself? A strong Heart allows us to engage in deeper reflection and achieve greater self-awareness. When we have a blocked Heart, then, how can we know for sure if we're as alright as we say we are?

Since our Heart is what lets us love unconditionally and connect with others, we can derive several telltale signs to determine when it's not flowing easily. When we feel disconnected from others, or unable to relate to them, it is a sign of an underactive Heart which has led us into isolation, and that is where it'll keep us unless we make a move to step outside once again.

When we are possessive, codependent, or self-negligent, it's an additional sign that our Heart is surely overactive; when our identity is so strongly invested in who we have, and what we can make them do for us, it shows that our Solar Plexus has taken a dive and our Heart is frantically burning out to try to make up the difference.

If you have urges to control others, or to use their love for you in order to attain power over them, then it is a sign that *all* your Chakras of Matter are off-balance in addition to your Heart. This urge to control comes from the belief that we are unable to generate soft, gentle, and loyal love in what we do, who we are, or how we live. This puts us into a terrible state of fear that can even drive one to become abusive in vain attempts to consolidate affection by force, trickery, and manipulation rather than an open, reciprocal exchange. Insomnia, weak immune systems, and higher blood pressure are also all signs of a troubled Heart, and manifest when our body can no longer hide the strain of a tortured soul.

Tragically, those who refuse to become abusers when all their Chakras of Matter are failing in this way will gradually lose the will to live instead.

Open and Breathe

Thankfully, this is not a binary choice between abuse and self-termination. It is fully possible for you to save yourself, and to regain a more open and affectionate connection with those you care about. For reawakening your Heart, the best starting move is to let go of vengeance.

You are not to be the judge, jury, and executioner of all the wrongs you've ever perceived in your life. As a great Taoist master once said, "He who substitutes the Master Executioner is like he who substitutes the Master Carpenter; rarely do they escape injury to themselves" (Lao Tzu & Wing, 1997, p. 173). When we continuously judge others, we make it more difficult for them to open up to us, ironically depriving us of the gentle love our Heart craves, leading to us creating our own hurt in the long run.

Aside from others, be more gentle with yourself. If you don't know how, first take note of all the things you say to yourself on a daily basis. Now, imagine you were saying these things to a child. Would you still dare to use such sharp words as blunt instruments against such an innocent soul? Your Heart, at its core, *is* innocent, no matter what you have done in life so far. It is the part of you that will always have the capacity to love and to care not because society demands it, but because it feels like the natural thing to do. Treat your Heart as if it were a child. Speak to it gently and kindly, and speak to yourself in this way, too. This doesn't mean blatantly ignoring your own shortcomings, but it does mean showing yourself patience; it means recognizing that you are still growing mentally and spiritually, and the best thing you can do when you stumble or err is simply to show yourself back to the correct path.

Never forget that; when you err off the path you feel you should be on, practice leading yourself back to it gently. Being overly harsh on yourself is like smacking someone face-down into the dirt for daring to step off the paving stones and onto the grass. Do not be like this to yourself. Just guide yourself back, and be open to the idea that among the grass lies a worthwhile path in itself.

When you settle down for the day and prepare to eat dinner, if you know your Heart is dormant and needs to be coaxed out of bed, consider going green. Spinach, green bell peppers, limes, and green apples can all help give your Heart the gentle kick it needs if you're truly struggling to express its energy. Aside from the apples, these foods are best imbibed in the form of a warm soup, often with foods that balance your lower three Chakras as well, as helping them stay open will do wonders for letting your Heart's force breathe.

Foods that synergize especially well are those that contain vitamin C, such as strawberries and citrus fruits. Vitamin C has a tendency to help the Heart reopen a bit, and the association of these foods with other Chakras (such as strawberries being associated with your Root) make for a great multi-pronged reawakening of your energy.

Chapter 6:

Your Throat

Your first Chakra of Energy, as well as your next stepping stone in interacting positively with the world, your Throat Chakra is a powerful force, intended to help you express your inner truth. When your lower Chakras are balanced, you develop a profound idea of what you want. Your Throat Chakra then helps ensure those wants are met in the most constructive way possible.

Those who study Chakras tend to see a strong link between the Sacral Chakra and the Throat Chakra, as while your Sacral is responsible for your creative drive, your Throat is what allows you to capture the truth through what you're creating. It is what allows you to express your intention with vivid clarity, and achieve consistent resonance with those around you. In Sanskrit, your Throat is under the name of *Visuddha*, which appropriately translates to "Especially Pure," as it is responsible for communicating the purest version of you. It can also be translated to "Antidote" or "Purifier," linking to the great healing effects that truth and authenticity can have in removing toxicity from a relationship, even if that truth isn't always easy to swallow.

While your Throat stands on its own like all Chakras, it also has strong links to your Heart and Solar Plexus. How can you set boundaries and establish a firm identity in the minds of those around you if you are not able to communicate exactly who you are? As for the Heart, your Throat is responsible not only for helping you be heard, but also helping you recognize when you are understood, and thus when it is alright for you to relax and listen. A healthy Throat can turn you into an active listener who'll speak to establish themselves, but will step down to make sure every other voice in the room gets the same chance. This chance, in turn, becomes an expression of unconditional love that feeds back into your Heart as well as your Throat.

To locate your Throat Chakra, feel the center of your neck. This is where it resides. Its energy, however, flows down as far as your shoulders, as well as your thyroid gland, impacting the energy of all forms of communication; it is not only the energy of your voice that is affected, but also the body language and hormonal energies of your physical form.

Symbols and Colors

When meditating on your Throat Chakra, the color you should envision is Blue. Its element is Ether or Space, which may seem ironic given that "in space, no one can hear you scream," but it emphasizes the wisdom that must accompany speech. Being a good speaker requires being a good listener, and one cannot be a good listener if one doesn't allow space to be filled. It also emphasizes that being heard isn't about making the most noise; even though making noise might get you attention, it won't necessarily bring anyone closer to understanding who you truly are.

The Throat's other symbols include the Sixteen-Petaled Lotus, as well as the Circle Within the Triangle, combining the shape associated with the Solar Plexus with what is often taken to be a full moon (compare and contrast the Circle of the Throat to the Crescent of the Sacral, the latter of which can be compared to a moon either waxing or waning).

When you wish to speak the mantra or seed-syllable for the Throat, say "Ham." Before you giggle too much, however, remember the way the "a" sound is supposed to be pronounced for these words; the mantra of "Ham" sounds much more like "hum" when spoken correctly. It is alright if you giggle, of course! It's just important when you wish to meditate seriously that you know to ask for focus to be on your Throat, rather than on a delicious meaty shank.

When you wish to make affirmations, or remind yourself of what is needed to maintain a healthy Throat, repeat to yourself, "I am an active listener. I focus not only on what I say, but also on what I hear during a conversation. I honor my voice and my inner truth, and permit it to speak. I am heard. I let go of any worries about what I think I "should have" said. What I say strives to be honest while respecting the balance of those around me. I communicate with clarity and empathy."

Balance in Your Throat: What to Strive For, and Signs of Blockage

Maintaining balance in one's Throat might feel like a tricky endeavor. It is a constant waltz between being honest and diplomatic, and many of us might struggle to be both simultaneously. When your Throat is in balance, however, you realize that these two things are not mutually exclusive. It is fully possible to be both at once, and it comes down to fearlessly expressing what you want while also intending not to hurt with your words.

C.S Lewis, of *Narnia* fame, expresses the importance of a balanced Throat in *The Screwtape Letters*, where at one point two devils share an exchange describing how people damn themselves through resentment and bottled-up rage when they do not freely speak their truths to one another. In the scenario of the book, this issue was evident in a formerly loving couple who kept making personal sacrifices for one another, but because they never communicated what they truly wanted, it just meant they both made themselves, and eventually each other, miserable without achieving anything.

This hopefully underscores the importance of keeping one's Throat Chakra open; you can have the most loving Heart in the world, but with a blocked Throat your loving energy could easily become pent-up and feel like a dammed river, frustrating your lower Chakras.

If you're unsure whether your Throat is in balance or not, there are three questions you can ask yourself about anything you have said, or wish to say. The first question is, "Are these words true?"

Pay careful attention to how you phrase yourself; you can still express subjective observations, feelings, and beliefs, but then you need to make sure that this is how you're framing your words; do not mistake your personal narrative for the universal narrative. This way, you can help your words be true, even when expressing strife or emotional turmoil.

The next question is, "Are these words needed?"

As a painter, I've found that if I try to capture every little detail of an object that I'm studying, then the message becomes unclear for my viewer. However, if I limit my brush strokes to define *only what is important to my message*, then my viewer will more readily understand my work. The same goes for speaking. Before talking, identify the crux behind your desire to talk in any given scenario, and open with it. Let people know exactly what you're getting at, or what you need, right off the bat. Do not mince words, otherwise you'll distract and confuse your listeners, meaning the conversation goes nowhere.

The final question is, "Are these words kind?"

Honesty and rudeness are not the same thing. I know plenty of honest people, and they're some of the gentlest individuals I know. I also know people who claim to be "honest" and all they've done is break others down at every opportunity, even contributing to one or two suicides among dear friends who absolutely didn't deserve to be broken down that way, as if our faults and weaknesses are our only truths; newsflash, they aren't.

Our successes and positive traits are just as true as our negative ones, if not more so since we ultimately define ourselves through what we accomplish, not through the failures we endured on our way to that accomplishment. To ensure your words are kind, let go of any beliefs you may have that hurting others will make them listen or get them to do what you want. Unless they're already broken and vulnerable, it won't work. And if they *are* already broken and vulnerable, it'd be better to use your Throat to build them back up into an emotionally functional human, not keep them under your thumb.

But I digress. If you've answered "yes" to the three questions above, and yet refused to speak your words, your Throat may be blocked. If you answered "no" at any point, yet spoke anyway, then your Throat may be blocked. If you are unsure whether to answer "yes" or "no" to "are they necessary?", then consider revisiting Chapter 4.

Note, however, that the state of blockage in your Throat is not a binary on/off thing. If you have a minor blockage, you might just have trouble speaking to certain people, like an in-law or an estranged friend. If you have a major blockage, however, you may find it difficult speaking to almost everybody.

Introversion is a common sign of a dormant Throat, and this is still something I struggle with from time to time today, but those who feel perpetually timid, unable to raise their voice above even a peep, have it far worse in that department. In extreme cases, one can even develop a fear of speaking up, which can become catastrophic when combined with an upset Root. It can mean feeling almost invisible.

When our Throat is off-balance through over-activity, however, such as when our Heart has shrunk, we tend to become poor listeners. We tend to come across as arrogant and supremely condescending in our tone, whether we choose to or not. We might even find ourselves tempted to gossip constantly, or murmur and criticize at every opportunity. In these cases, reopening your Heart may help, but the methods for reopening your Throat will make a difference both for the dormant and for the over-active.

If you still aren't sure that your Throat is blocked, further telltale psychological signs include lacking the vocabulary to describe thoughts, emotions, or ideas, especially if they're deeply relevant to you in either a personal or professional context. Likewise, if you feel like you are keeping an excessive number of secrets, or if you feel that no one understands who you truly are deep down, you may have a blocked Throat.

Physical signs include a stiff neck, sore throat, and anomalous fluctuations in your hormone levels.

Open and Speak

As you might imagine, expanding your vocabulary is a great way to awaken your Throat, the corollary being that living in a country where your language isn't commonly spoken is a great way for your Throat to close. Reading and consuming media in the language of your neighbors, then, can help you open your Throat back up. However, reading alone isn't quite enough. After all, reading is one of the favorite pastimes of many introverts, and yet by definition their Throat is still closed (albeit only to a very minor degree if they nonetheless feel comfortable and secure in who they are).

If you'll allow me to speculate, I like to think that their passion for reading is a subconscious move to help their Throat re-awaken, and certainly such individuals light up rapidly when they find someone with similar knowledge and interests, but if you wish to progress past introversion, or at least do not wish to feel held back by it in social situations, the next step in awakening your Throat involves the practice of speech.

What does this mean? Consider the choir. Before putting on a dazzling performance, a choir will first practice an array of warm-up exercises to help their vocal cords become smooth and to build up their confidence. In reality, they're ensuring their Throats are open for the performance. Likewise, many comedians and stage performers have a warm-up act such as the infamously classic "aristocrats" skit that they'll share with their peers backstage as a way to ensure that their Throat Chakras are clear, guaranteeing their live performance will be the best hit it can be.

If even professional performers must practice like this to ensure their expression flows smoothly, perhaps you should do the same. Instead of just reading in your head when you pick up a book, read aloud. Children do this to help learn the words, but you are doing this instead to master them, and how they might roll off your tongue. The more you practice speaking, the easier it becomes.

If you have something specific on your mind that is nonetheless very difficult to say, it is best to write out what it is, and then practice it. The tone you wish to aim for in these cases shouldn't be confrontative, nor should it be simpering. Simply make it to the point while taking into account any explicit pleasantries or customs that you are aware of. Do not invent pleasantries or customs, as this will obscure your message and lead to confusion. It may also help to figure out what you will say when the worst happens, such as being rejected or ignored, but take care not to overplan; map out too many preset responses, and it might lead to an overactive Throat, impairing your ability to listen and respond sensitively to the individual you're dealing with.

If this all sounds like a bit much, perhaps it'll help to step outside and clear your head. This is something many people do, and by now you already know the benefits being outdoors can have on your lower Chakras, but when it is a cloudless day, the outdoors become a heaven for your Throat. On a cloudless day, you can look right up into space, the element of your Throat, and take in its energies. This doesn't have to be at night; you do not need to be able to see the moon or the stars. Space is always above us, far beyond the atmosphere we breathe in, and on a clear, sunny day the ether can reach out to us with minimal obstruction.

To further aid your Throat, you can immerse yourself in the scents of rosemary, peppermint, cypress, or roman chamomile. Most of these come in the form of teas, which allows you to let their steam waft over your neck and shoulders before you pour the contents down your throat. For pure potent aroma, however, you'll want to have these substances in essential oil form instead; essential oils have naturally potent scents, so you do not need to worry about doing anything special to benefit from them other than applying them to the fabrics in your living area. Unlike the tea version, of course, you cannot imbibe these in essential oil form; it wouldn't be safe.

What you should ingest, however, are blueberries, which are said to help boost receptiveness and confidence when taken in advance preparation of a challenging conversation. You can even combine them with blackberries and coconuts for a mixed snack or blend all three for a sweet fruit shake that'll aid some of your lower Chakras as well. For more savory meals, any food can be made to help serve your Throat Chakra if you add a little salt, lemongrass, or ginger to season it. Such simple spices enhance flavor without obscuring it, and are linked with the ability to speak clearly and expressively without muddying your message.

Finally, back to fruits, aside from blueberries your best options are any fruit that grows on a tree and falls to the ground when it is ready to be eaten. This is because their tendency to fall only when they're ready symbolizes authenticity; fruits do not offer themselves up to anyone when they do not yet have anything to give, instead choosing to be patient and letting their development occur naturally. In this way, those who wish for an open Throat should be more like the fruit, and the consumption of such fruit carries a strong symbolic meaning that can help give you the psychological boost you need.

Chapter 7:

Your Third Eye

You have become acquainted with so many of your Chakras, and now we finally reach your second Chakra of Energy, your Third Eye. Unlike your previous Chakras, your Third Eye only begins to become a significant factor in your life as you transition into adolescence; perhaps this is why, in addition to the physical and hormonal changes that occur during this time, one might have felt so strange as one transitioned into adulthood. Yet from that point onwards, your Third Eye stays with you for the rest of your life. It is similar to your Solar Plexus in that it requires conviction to run smoothly. It is also similar to your Sacral in that it can be waylaid by doubting your potential value as an individual.

As we go through life, it is not uncommon that we end up creating convictions that undermine our self-image and general feelings of self-worth. This creates a paradox, one where you have the conviction needed for a healthy Third Eye, yet that conviction has been turned against it through the excessive reproduction of doubt. The irony is that your Third Eye is responsible for helping you see through illusions, cut through obfuscations, and readily distinguish fantasy from reality, yet it is this excessive doubt that can cause it to go astray, and even fall asleep. Your Third Eye will always do its best to reassure you when you're feeling uneasy or upset, but when you do not listen, or if you keep giving it the same negative story over and over again, it eventually stops speaking, allowing internal lies to multiply.

This energy center is positioned in the center of your brow, and is closely linked to your pineal gland in your brain, which is responsible for your sleep cycle.

Why would our Third Eye be linked to our pineal gland? Because the quality of our sleep can often be the deciding factor in telling the truth from the lie. The more tired we are, the slower our thoughts become, and the longer they take to spot inconsistencies or achieve full comprehension of a situation. Part of the reason that sleep deprivation is considered such a cruel thing to inflict on another is because it hinders their ability to tell fact from fiction. Healthy sleep, then, is the first step towards a healthy Third Eye. But it does not stop there, as you'll shortly find in this chapter.

In Sanskrit, this Chakra is known as *Ajna*, which can be translated as "to observe," "to notice," or even "to lead." Without this Chakra being in balance, you cannot easily discern the true nature of a person, nor the true meaning of their words. Nor will you have an easy time distinguishing your own beliefs or personal truths for things that are objectively real or universally true for everyone. When your Third Eye is in balance, however, not only will you gain these abilities, but through these abilities you'll also gain both an enhanced ability to master yourself, as well as the credibility needed to inspire trust and attain command over others.

It is rather apt, then, that *Ajna* can translate both into seeing and into commanding.

Symbols and Colors

Out of all the Chakras, this one's mantra syllable is the most readily recognized in popular culture, the classic "Ohm" that actors will utter when their character is supposed to be meditating. The correct way to write it, however, is as "Aum" or "Om." "Ohm" may be correct phonetically, but when spelled this way it is a unit of electrical resistance, rather than a focusing word for your inner intuition.

Your Third Eye Chakra takes on a powerful indigo hue. Its symbols are the Two-Petaled Lotus, and its shape is an upside-down Triangle like your Solar Plexus. Your Chakras are at times like poetry, and here we see the symbol for identity repeat once more yet in a different context. From Solar Plexus to Third Eye, you move from developing belief in yourself to recognizing the truth in yourself, a process which isn't always easy.

The element of your Third Eye is the very essence of light itself; everything that your eyes can see could potentially contribute to your Third Eye, especially when viewed under natural light, while pitch black would by contrast distress it. Your Third Eye adores the gentle interplay of natural shadow and light, while simultaneously despising extreme darkness. At night, it falls in love with the stars and longs for the moon.

Your Third Eye additionally receives support from each of the elements oscillating out of your lower Chakras, which is good because your Third Eye has one of the hardest jobs of the lot. It is never easy to discern the truth, especially when we find truth uncomfortable. It is no surprise, then, that while it is natural for all of our Chakras to go off-balance from time to time, the Third Eye tends to do it most. Do not feel ashamed, then, if you find yourself having to rebalance it more frequently than your other Chakras.

When you wish to focus on reaffirming the beauty and good your Third Eye can do, use sentences such as, "I forgive myself, I am at peace, I am the source of my own truth and love. I listen to the advice I offer myself, I nurture my soul and I strive to learn from all my experiences, whether I perceived them to be good or bad at the time."

If any of this sounds familiar, then it's probably because all of these affirmations resonate in some way with one of your previous Chakras. Your Third Eye isn't just about seeing the truth in the world around you, it's about recognizing the truth in yourself, even right down to your other Chakras. If an affirmation ever feels untrue to you, either adjust it so that it fits you more honestly, or strive to live to the original affirmation's ideals. This is a choice that only you can make. All one can ask is that you not be afraid to choose that which will bring you long-lasting happiness.

Keeping Your Third Eye Wide Open

It should be noted immediately that if your Root or Sacral Chakras were neglected in your early life, your Third Eye may have had a stunted start when you finally hit puberty. It is difficult to see the truth when, at our cores, we are taught to accept the falsehoods that we're worthless, that we do not belong upon this world, or that we are or are unable to contribute anything of value. In fact, one of the greatest challenges of your Third Eye lies in spotting and uprooting these deep-seated limiting beliefs.

However, it is difficult to spot such things when we're complacent. When you were young, did your family or peer group encourage free thought? Did they promote exposure to new ideas, or make it fun to revisit and dissect old ones? Were they great people to debate and discuss ideas with? Or were you conditioned to avoid questioning, to keep silent instead of asking difficult questions? Were you forced to hide and suppress your doubts, rather than lay them out in the open to be dealt with in a healthy and informative manner?

The general rule when it comes to the Third Eye is that those who are practiced at critically examining ideas, both internally and externally, will experience greater balance in this Chakra, while those who are constantly conditioned to follow beliefs blindly will be off-balance or experience dormancy in this Chakra.

Contrary to what some may believe, having faith and following something blindly are not the same thing. It is possible to be deeply religious and have a powerful Third Eye, and it is possible to be strictly secular, believing nothing beyond what is scientifically measurable, and yet have a dormant Third Eye. This is because, despite benefiting from critical thinking, the Third Eye is not about cold, hard logic per se, but rather about awareness; it focuses our powers of intuition, imagination, and self-awareness to let us accurately grasp concepts that exist outside of the very limited information humanity currently has. This can mean something as complex as an ancient faith, or something as simple as one's personal conscience.

One way or the other, our Third Eye is what allows us to trust in what we cannot yet confirm and, when used for good, it lets us trust in ideas that bring us comfort, joy, and meaning. It also lets us test and critique those ideas where they matter, so that our relationship with our beliefs can grow and mature into something real and practical, something that can make a meaningful positive impact on the world around us through our actions, rather than remain a pie in the sky.

It keeps our perspectives broad, reminding us that our view of the universe is still so much smaller than the universe itself. Through this, one gains a new lens through which to self-reflect.

It should be clarified that challenging your current beliefs does not equate to doubting yourself.

When you update the drivers on your computer, are you saying your computer is not good enough? When you learn something new, are you saying you're not good enough? Of course not! It's just a fact of life that the more informed you are, the better a position you're in to make decisions, and the more smoothly things flow for you in challenging situations. This is on the personal scale.

On the grand scale, consider that the longest-lasting traditions, beliefs we often take for granted as being immortal, are those that are not afraid to question themselves and then adapt in the face of new circumstances, such as the tradition of knighthood, which went from a military rank to a social and cultural accolade, while still preserving its vital core of honor, dignity, and merit. Compare and contrast to the feudal system that knighthood originated from, which detached from the hearts and minds of the people and then faded away because it couldn't accommodate the ever-changing socio-political needs of those living under it. A balanced Third Eye lets you intuitively sense whether to stand your ground or move forward; it tells the difference between conviction and stagnation, as well as the difference between progression and aimlessness.

When you can maintain faith in yourself, while being fearless in challenging what you place conviction in, you allow your awareness to continuously reach out, aiding your Throat and Heart while maintaining your sense of the bigger picture in life. When your Third Eye is in balance, you do not get caught up in the minutiae of what people say. You do not pick apart their sentences word by word because, in the same way that people are not entirely what they create and are not entirely what they believe, they are not entirely what they speak. What a person believes is based on the information they have and the habits they have formed, what they speak is based on how they're feeling, and what they create is based on the means that they have available.

A balanced Third Eye looks past all this to help you get to the core of a person, a powerful ability that allows one to attain peace and save it from the maw of terrible conflict. A balanced Third Eye recognizes that most of us aren't exactly social butterflies or masters of presentation by any means, and thus lets its intuition guide you in treating others according to a compassionate and empathic baseline, rather than according to the surface-level veneer they present themselves with. Remember, in Chapter 4 we covered how your character is like an iceberg; do you not think that may be true for those around you as well?

In contrast, an imbalanced or dormant Third Eye is paranoid, finding fear, drama, and conflict in places where it doesn't exist; every word from another feels like a slight, every silence a judgement, and every compliment a damnation by faint praise.

When one's Third Eye is dormant, one often uses the imagination not to dream or create, but to try to escape a reality that has been obscured by one's self-defeating narrative to such a grievous degree that sanity no longer seems possible without illusion. Even the more logical among us tend to get lost in our own thoughts when our Third Eye is off-key, even at the most inappropriate times such as in the middle of a conversation, or while trying to operate a vehicle, causing anything from extended digressions to heart wrenching thought-spirals.

The worse the unbalancing becomes, the more extreme the signs grow. In the most extreme cases, one can become ruthlessly outcome-orientated, yet simultaneously cripplingly indecisive. We then struggle to connect to others on a deeper level, often because we mistakenly believe that this depth isn't there.

Whether we're emotional or logical, when our Third Eye is drastically off-balance we enter a state of extreme; we either become a turbulent maelstrom of drama and draining energy, or we become cold, utilitarian, and numb in our detachment.

Without a balanced Third Eye, we struggle to balance our emotion and reason to effectively accomplish our goals and maintain our connections, causing ourselves endless frustration. Stress, overwhelming mental clutter, and an abstract mental "fog" soon follow for an overactive Chakra, while loss of concentration and a deep-seated fear of new ideas follows an underactive one.

For chronically imbalanced Third Eyes, expect physical pain in the form of constant headaches, sinus pain and, unsurprisingly, eye pains.

Awaken

To help your Third Eye stay open, the best thing you can do is keep a journal. We mentioned journals earlier in Chapter 3 due to their excellent use as a medium for creative expression. For your Third Eye, however, it is more important that you write with the intention of self-reflection. Try to imagine what you look like to those around you. Do not take anything about yourself for granted; assume this is the first time they've seen you. Examine how you behave. How do you come across? Cold, busy, anxious, cross? How would you feel if you had to deal with someone like that? Do those around you seem to feel the same way? If you ever feel unsure, it helps to speak openly with those you can trust, as hearing another human being's perspective without immediately passing judgement on it is a great way to help your Third Eye awaken.

Do not criticize what this person is saying to you, but if you have a question or if at any time something seems unclear; ask about it. Call for clarity, and give them a chance to explain. Do not underestimate what they know, what they've been through, or what they might carry in their heart. Again, remember what we said about icebergs. Encourage the person speaking to you to reveal more of their thoughts from beneath the surface. Give them space to speak, and lead them down mental pathways that they're happy to dive into. When a person is enabled to speak passionately and feel heard while doing so, all sorts of gems can come out. The true beauty of this is that while their perspective may help your Third Eye, through choosing them to do this you also help their Throat. No matter where we are in relation to one another in developing our Chakras, we can all give each other a helping hand when given both the chance and a patient heart.

Beyond this, do not be afraid to let the topic drift away from being about you. The next best thing you can do is examine multiple viewpoints on a topic or issue. This could mean examining how two different political parties relate to a social challenge, different religions view divinity, different scientists give hypotheses to explain an observation, or different cultures view a historic event. It may feel a little weird at first, but shaking the mould of your comfort zone is key to keeping your Third Eye open.

The next best thing is to write down all your core beliefs, both positive and negative, and ask, "Is that actually true?"

This will quickly help you decide what truly matters to you among your convictions, as well as help you see how you've grown and developed since you first made them. Do not be stingy in your research; go online to find supporting viewpoints for your beliefs, as well as critiques that highlight possible flaws. If you feel insecure, unworthy of life, or worthy of unending punishment, these are all great core beliefs to start with. Debunking them can be one of the most cathartic experiences one can have, and may turn out to be as simple, yet as difficult, as dealing with unresolved grief in your life.

Dietary choices that support opening and focusing your Third Eye include dark chocolate, walnuts, chia seeds, salmon, or sardines. For chocolate, this is because it's a source of magnesium and serotonin, the former of which reduces stress and simplifies grief, while the latter helps lift off unwarranted feelings of despondency. For the walnuts et al, it's due to their great omega-3 content. Omega-3 is a great cognitive booster, which helps you reason effectively, a vital ability when trying to make gains with your Third Eye. Other than that, any indigo or near-indigo foods such as blackberries, blueberries, red grapes, aubergines and the like are good supplements as they help you envision the color needed to focus on your Third Eye during meditation.

Chapter 8:

Your Crown Chakra

Your third Chakra of Energy, as well as your final Chakra in the stream of divine energy coursing through your spine, is your Crown Chakra. If your Root is what keeps you grounded in life on Earth, your Crown is what allows you to find meaning in the heavens above. Unlike your Third Eye, Throat and other lower Chakras, your Crown does not hold the trappings of intellectualism, nor is it really that concerned with the acquisition of *things*, whether those things be stockpiles of resources, relationships, honors, accolades, fame, or glory. It enjoys learning, but isn't concerned so much with academicism. It cares not for titles, marks, or prizes, but simply for growth, and a sense of unity. Out of all your Chakras, this one is your most fluid, constantly moving in a flux through each day of your life since your heart began to beat. As such, even experts on Chakra energy will not have their Crown active all the time, even though they may be able to keep theirs open for longer.

In Sanskrit, this Chakra was written down as *Sahaswara* or *Sahasrara,* which simply translates to "One-Thousand-Petaled Lotus." This Chakra is said to be our link between our physical selves and the Divine, between our tiny little self and the near-infinite universe around us. Its Sanskrit name, then, helps underscore the sheer scale of what our Crown connects us to, as its lotus is given several hundred times more petals than the rest of our Chakras combined. It is like connecting our minds and voices to a network of thousands.

As mystical as this sounds, however, the Crown's benefits aid is in invaluable ways, often without us realizing. This is the Chakra that motivates us to act and to create our masterpieces, to push us beyond creating for the sake of food or recognition, to push us beyond creating for the sake of obvious gain. This Chakra is what gives us our *inspiration*, our ability to comprehend and act on ideas of such unique flavor and such natural synergy with the world around us that they empower us to create something overflowing with evidence of love and care. This Chakra is what allows us to see beauty in the world around us, as well as bring more beauty into it. Our Crown is what allows us to create works that resonate with the hearts of generations, of those who are not only around you now, but also those who are still to come. Even the most secular individual can therefore benefit from an active Crown because it enables them to add that special, undefinable masterstroke to their work, while those of a more spiritual bent have the added benefit of feeling a greater degree of closeness to their deity.

When our Crown is active and alive, we begin to gain a profound understanding of cause and effect. We see our world as a pond, with every action we take a pebble that casts out ripples across the water. We see how the ripples of one pebble interact with those of another, how the collision and superposition can end up affecting the shape of the water even at the opposite end of the pond, far away from where the initial splashes occurred. We begin to see how these movements build and overlap across one another.

Eventually, we begin to realize that everything that exists right now, whether it is the solar energy of a decaying star, or a cluster of spawning tadpoles, is interdependent. What happens to one can cause a chain reaction to affect the other, whether that be physically as tadpoles experience a pleasant day thanks to the gravitational equilibrium of our galaxy, or conceptually as stars become purposeless when they don't have life to appreciate them.

Appropriately for a Chakra so concerned with the heavens and the universe above, this energy wheel sits at the very top of your head—not your forehead, but rather right on the mostly flat, slightly curved bit that you'd fit your hat on.

Symbols and Colors

As you can guess, the One-Thousand-Petaled Lotus is one of the main symbols of this Chakra. As you may have noticed, the colors progress like a rainbow. You may also be able to guess that this Chakra's energy is violet. But what is its element? It is Thought. However, not any old thought will do. Otherwise, overthinking wouldn't be an issue, and we'd never con or fool ourselves through logical fallacies or one-sided introspection. No, this Chakra's element is Thought, but only if all your other Chakras are already in alignment. The more Chakras you have that are off-balance, the more mangled and garbled your thought becomes as it contends with all your blockages, and thus the less useful Thought will be for keeping your Crown active. An alternate element is Cosmic Energy, but in practice this'll only mean spending more time in sunlight, which is something previous Chakras already cover.

When you wish to focus your meditations on your Crown, however, you'll be delighted to know that this Chakra's seed-syllable is a rather relieved-sounding "Ah," and its affirmations include statements such as, "We are all on this planet to make a difference," or, "I am love, I am life, I am light. I am joy," or even, "In this moment, I am secure. At this moment, I feel in tune with Creation. In this moment I can both perceive and accept the beauty of this world; the flawed gem that it is, it is still beautiful. It is my pleasure to find others with love to share, and give their energies an inroad into my life."

Although the Crown's element may be harder to properly harness, on the bright side affirmations tend to have a significantly more powerful effect on it. This is because an open Crown requires one to be at ease with oneself, and to have a healthy, full yet unbloated self-esteem. All affirmations aid in this.

Your Crown: a Flawed Gem

Our Crowns allow our awareness to ascend to a higher plane of observation and reasoning. It lets us keep our deepest desires close to our heart, allowing us to form strategies to their fulfillment without the burden of clutter or avarice. In this way, our Crown forms our conscience, our moral compass which guides us along our optimal path to the best of its ability.

However, when our Crowns are off-balance, we struggle to gauge what we need, or even what we really want. Because of this, we begin to reach out to everything we can lay our hands on, accumulating hoards of knick-knacks and bric-a-brac "just in case" it turns out to be useful to us later on, all the while being willfully oblivious to how much of our energy and vital strategic resources (e.g. money) we are wasting on all these unnecessary acquisitions.

In the long run, such behavior encourages greed. The more we carry with us in our life, the bigger our house needs to be to hold it all. The bigger our house needs to be, the more we need to earn each month to pay it off. The more we need to earn each month, the more we have to face the difficult choice of working longer hours and burning ourselves out, or leaving others by the wayside as we focus on optimizing profits through any means we are able to...as long as it doesn't involve giving up any of the useless clutter that's making us work this hard.

One doesn't realize how damaging this process can be to a soul until it causes a family unit to break down, or a relationship to end, or an important event to be missed, such as the last days of one's grandmother or the crowning achievement of a best friend. At this point, do you even remember what your original goal even was? It's too often that we spend so much time chasing things, when what we really wanted was a meaningful connection with a *person* instead. Sometimes, it's a specific person that we might never be able to replace.

Whenever your Crown unbalances, do your best to be as self-aware of the above tendencies as possible, so that you may catch yourself before you drift too far away from what you love, chasing green bait, shiny lures, and dazzling lights. For greater help in this matter, I recommend investigating the topic of Minimalism, a belief system dedicated to curbing the self-destructive tendencies of frivolous and insensitive spending.

Aside from greed or vulnerability to unnecessary degrees of materialism, a dormant Crown can also make it difficult for us to find our inspiration, or can even make us feel suddenly powerless or incompetent at something we're normally one of the best at. We might still perform well, yet we find our work lacks that spark, or that special zing that made it resonate with both us and those around us. Without that zing, our passions begin to feel more like chores. With that spark, however, even our chores can be woven into our passions. A mind without inspiration is inclined to oversleep, while a mind with inspiration will devote every waking moment to what it truly loves, as well as to what will add value to the world. Therefore, a working Crown is an invaluable assistant to anyone who wishes to make meaningful contributions to their field, or who wishes to make the most they can out of each day.

Like with all of our other Chakras, however, it is also possible to *overfeed* our Crowns. This is a common pitfall one can tumble into, especially if one has been doing very well so far in balancing the other Chakras. When we do well, we are faced with the temptation to feel superior, to feel elite, as if we're somehow inherently above the people we share this planet with. However, it is this very feeling of superiority that creates barriers between us and the universe that our Crown needs to connect with. A balanced Crown means recognizing that you are a *part* of creation, not *above* it. Although you may be more valuable in some situations or in some fields than those around you, this does not inherently mean that you're more worthy of life. For the altruistic, the idea is that you build yourself up, treat yourself well, and then extend that energy out to others. Giving room to others to learn and grow can lead to a deep sense of personal freedom.

For the pragmatic, however, it should be noted that when your Crown is overfed to the point that you feel inherently superior, you'll also begin to weaken and exhaust yourself because you will expend your time and effort on tasks better suited for those around you. Even if you do delegate, an overfed ego might still cause you to missassign those who wish to work for you, as you'll treat them more like extensions of your will than as individuals with their own in-depth skill sets, talents, experiences, and biases. You will battle to coordinate, both when it comes to teams and when it comes to your own hand-eye interaction.

"If you want something done right, do it yourself" thus becomes the mantra of those with overactive Crowns, as they continuously fail to match people to the tasks they love, only considering one's own needs. This degradation of critical understanding and awareness beyond the self can become fatal when it causes you to become haughty; to become so sure of your own abilities that you fail to assess your competition, fail to plan contingencies for situations you can control, and fail to even determine whether or not a situation *can* be controlled by you, or whether it is bigger than that and requires aid from outside.

Self-destructive tendencies such as this are hallmarks of an overactive Crown, despite the huge ego such overactivity tends to create.

Other telltale signs include having total apathy for anything that doesn't directly impact your life, as well as struggling to let go of things you no longer need, or people who might wish for more time on things that do not involve you. This links back to the flaws of greed and hoarding that were mentioned earlier this chapter.

Seating Your Crown

At several points in this book, we have mentioned how going outdoors can be good for balancing the Chakras. This applies to the Crown, too, but requires you to adopt a certain mindset. You do not need to be in nature for this, but it's preferred that you are on foot. As you move about through the world, do your best to observe all that is around you. Gauge your emotional response to each person or thing you encounter on your journey. As you do so, challenge yourself to feel a sense of unity with what you encounter, without feeling possessive over it, without presuming to fully understand it, and without presuming to be entirely in sync with it. You do not need to be these things, simply acknowledge that you are coexisting with what is around you now. Acknowledge that, were any of this to stop existing, life would be subtly different in ways that one cannot foresee.

If you encounter someone you know, or are deeply familiar with, the rules are still the same, although you can take your acknowledgements to a more personal level by experiencing gratitude for all that this person has added to your life, as well as being conscious of the fact that even when they aren't around you, they still have the right, the energy, and the potential to add similar value to this world you both live in.

A loving spouse, for instance, can and should still be allowed to add love to all the world around them. Even though you're the only one they kiss so passionately on the mouth, the only one whose arms they'll fall asleep in, love comes in many more forms than that. It comes in care and attention, and their sharing care with another doesn't diminish the value of the care they reserve for you.

As you're walking about, try to elevate yourself. Find a hill to hike up, so that the town you live in becomes a grand vista for you to take in, and all its inhabitants look like ants. To help your Crown unblock, recognize that none of those people are ants; in fact, you could be any one of them, and might even look like one to someone who is even higher up. Yet, that perspective is brought about by distance, not by power. Take care as you grow that your power never becomes an excuse to create distance. Distance is only for when you cannot get any nearer to a person without shutting down your Heart, and even then only so that you can still show love in some small way from where you're still standing.

The next way to help your Crown unblock is through parting with things that are only weighing you down; with things that are not making a meaningful contribution to your overall goals. To help decide what these items are, first start by marking off and giving away anything you haven't used in the past year. Then, for things that do not include professional tools, start marking off and giving away anything you haven't used in the last three months. Then, when you're ready and feeling more certain, within the last three weeks. This doesn't have to be all at once. If you're only willing to part with things you haven't used in only a year, stick with that, even if you do so for several years before feeling ready to move onto the next stage. Be patient with yourself. This process isn't actually about giving things away, it is simply about recognizing what you really need in life, and that can take time.

When giving away, this includes parting with redundancies of items you'd otherwise keep (e.g. your twelfth pair of cutlery when you're only a family of four and you almost never have more than eight visitors at once). Be sure to look out for better ways to achieve items that do currently fulfill a goal (e.g. instead of keeping a box of sentimental items that you never use, rather photograph them and upload them on Google Drive so that you can keep the memories, the most important part of a sentimental item, while freeing yourself up to give the actual physical object away). Finally, everything you own says something about you. Make sure that what these objects are saying is true.

When you wish to unblock your Crown through the power of dietary planning, herbal teas and ginger tend to be best thanks to their cleansing properties, while any naturally violet food will help thanks to being a visual stimulation of the Crown's color.

Chapter 9:

Balance and Heal Your Chakras

By now, you should have a fair idea of how to balance each of your Chakras, as well as help them heal. However, one understands that it can be tricky to decide which Chakra to begin with, especially since our energies are in a constant state of flux, ebbing and flowing, making concrete decisions difficult. For this reason, I've included a short questionnaire to help you be more swift and decisive in your healing, as well as an easy-to-read segment on the different healing methods, all in one place, including methods we haven't discussed much in previous chapters.

Chakra Triage

Although most of us have several Chakras in need of help at any one time, we don't always have the time and energy to address them all with the same level of care. To determine which Chakra needs your love and attention most, ask yourself the following:

What's the most important thing to you that you HAVEN'T had in your life lately?

1. Safety and stability
2. The ability to create and nurture
3. Identity and integrity
4. Empathy
5. Comprehension
6. Intuition and planning
7. Inspiration or spiritual fulfillment

What are you struggling the most with?

1. Eating disorders, depression, general insecurity
2. Coping with change, achieving sexual fulfillment, creating something worthwhile
3. Sticking to my decisions, figuring out who I am
4. Overcoming abuse or toxicity in my personal relationships, achieving independence in my relationships, believing I am worth loving
5. Getting the courage to ask for what I need, avoiding zoning out while listening to another
6. Trusting others, believing the best in people, taking advantage of changing situations to achieve outcomes that are different from what I planned yet still favorable or advantageous
7. A deep feeling of disconnection, or depression, but I feel secure in my right to love and exist

What do you wish for most these days?

1. A meaningful career, the means to provide for myself and those I care for
2. A healthier sex life and a potent creative flow
3. Self-confidence and control over my direction in life
4. A healthier connection with others, self-acceptance
5. I wish people understood what I was on about!
6. Better overall judgement
7. Inner peace, spiritual connection, "Eureka!" moments

Which affirmation is the LEAST true for you?

1. I am safe
2. I am creative and lively
3. I know who I am and want I want, and I possess the courage and personal power to pursue my goals
4. I demonstrate empathic love to both myself and to those around me
5. I am able to clearly communicate my perspective, and allow others to speak theirs
6. My gut feelings are almost always helpful or correct
7. I feel connected to my better self, as well as to life as a whole

Which kind of ailment (if any) is a constant bother to you?

1. Eating disorders, constipation, kidney troubles, lower back pains
2. Troubles with my lower sexual organs and/or urinary tract
3. Skin diseases, indigestion
4. Respiratory or circulatory issues, upper back pain
5. Voice loss, thyroid issues, pain in the neck/ shoulder/ jaw, tonsillitis
6. Headaches, audio-visual issues, dizziness
7. Airheadedness, painful sensitivity to light

Which color is the LEAST compelling for you right now?

1. Red
2. Orange
3. Yellow
4. Green
5. Blue
6. Indigo
7. Violet or White

Results

If you answered 1 for the majority of the above questions, then your Root is in most urgent need of care. 2 would be your Sacral, 3 your Solar Plexus and so forth, with your Crown naturally being 7 If multiple Chakras tie for "most urgent," start with the *Meditation* exercise below, as that'll help you strengthen your focus in addition to gaining its healing properties. Otherwise, continue on with any healing method you wish.

How to Heal

Meditation

While the basic meditation technique from Chapter 1 is great for clearing your mind, and the mantras and symbols you've learned in each of the later chapters can help hone your focus, I think we're ready for something more advanced; something that will heal and balance, rather than simply awaken. The following is intended to be a flexible meditation script to help you perform deeper cleaning on all your Chakras in one session. It is recommended that you follow the full script until you feel more balanced and sure of yourself, from which point you can pick and choose which Chakras you work on in any given setting.

The Next Step in Meditation

To begin your healing meditation, begin as you would according to the method in Chapter 1. If you want, you can put on some soothing ambience as you settle in, but do not visualize any shapes or colors yet.

After a few minutes of feeling mentally clear, envision white light coming from the core of the Earth, working its way through the ground until it taps into the base of your spine. Imagine this bright energy working its way up your spine until it reaches the top of your head, and flows out into the universe beyond. If you're having trouble visualizing this flow, then instead picture it the opposite way; visualize bright cosmic light coming down from the heavens, entering through your head, and working its way down your back to the base of your spine and into the ground. Regardless of the direction you can see, maintain that vision, but begin to focus on the white light around your Root.

Begin to visualize that this white light isn't moving in a straight line, but is actually spinning in a circle at your tailbone as it passes through you. Imagine it turning a deep crimson as it spins. How does that energy feel to you? How does it react when you breathe? Visualize how any old or rotten energies get released as you breathe in and out deeply, how the crimson becomes cleaner. Encourage it to spin more and more, like you'd encourage a child to keep spinning the wheels of a bicycle, until it spins on its own.

From there, move your mind into a space just below your belly button, where your Sacral is. Picture how the white light is spinning around there, and see how beautifully orange it turns as it does so. With the depth of your breath, clean this center, and visualize the streams in and out becoming unblocked. When it begins to spin effortlessly on its own, you can move onto your Solar Plexus, about an inch *above* your navel.

This is one of your most vibrant Chakras. As you picture its spinning energy turning yellow, visualize that yellow filling up your entire being and radiating into the environment around you, but make sure you don't upset the spinning of your lower Chakras as you do so.

When your Solar Plexus is now spinning on its own, move onto your Heart. Imagine that the very air you breathe in is turning a cool, fertile green as it enters into your lungs and oxygenates the blood passing through your body. See the circle of energy spinning in your chest, see how vivid that green light becomes as you keep feeding it life and oxygen. Try to expand that green light so that it fills your whole being, but again without stepping on the toes of your Chakras below. Encourage coexistence within yourself. You may place your hand over your Heart should you feel the urge to do so.

Now, your Throat. Imagine this center of energy sitting in the hollow of your neck, except it is not blocking your path. Rather, it is facilitating it, like a smooth road along which your words can travel. Imagine a blue light where it spins, and visualize your breath turning a brilliant blue as you exhale, as if imbued with the energy of truth and tranquility. See your Throat Chakra spin naturally with every breath you take.

Almost there. Your Third Eye is potent and deep, yet simple. Simply imagine a wheel of light spinning in the middle of your brow, and see it turn a deeper and deeper shade of indigo as you encourage it to spin faster and faster.

When it can spin on its own, move onto your Crown, picturing a bright beam of purple light radiating out into the universe around you. This is the energy you give back out to the heavens and earth that sustains you.

From this point, let your muscles relax completely, releasing all tension, and in your mind's eye see your body without the flesh and bone, but just with the light and colors of your Chakras. Watch how the colors pulse as you breathe.

Now that you've completed this basic procedure, you'll find it easier to revisit specific Chakras as needed.

What If I Cannot Get All My Wheels Spinning - Revisiting Chakras

As you've worked through each of your Chakras, you may have felt uncomfortable visualizing a specific center, or even found it difficult imagining its movement at all. This is where your current blockages lie. To clear it through meditation, focus on it like you did in the exercise above, but only pay attention to that specific Chakra. Place your hand over its area. Draw more and more bright white light from reality around you into that specific point while simultaneously visualizing the removal of toxins from there. Focus your energy on making that Chakra's wheel spin faster and faster as the energy pours in, as if you're using a combination of lubrication and torsion to unstick a gear. The greater the blockage, the more time and energy will need to be applied, so do not be afraid to be patient with yourself.

To make things easier, do not forget to employ that Chakra's mantra syllable as you work your healing through meditation.

Affirmations

We've already covered affirmations quite extensively in the beginning of each Chakra's chapter, so here is a general overview along with some extra tips to help you create your own.

Firstly, seed syllables and affirmations can be used almost interchangeably if you're meditating alone. Remembering seven syllables, one for each Chakra, can certainly be faster and easier than having to recite entire sentences. However, affirmations still provide a great source of conscious focus, a focus that not everyone finds in seed syllables. Sentence-length affirmations also retain effectiveness when spoken in front of a mirror, which some may prefer.

The most effective affirmations, however, are the ones that are deeply personal to you. If affirmations from previous chapters no longer resonate with you, here is what you need to know to determine your own:

1. In general, affirmations are "I can" or "I am" statements. They define you based on what you are, what you have, or what you can control, no matter how great or small these things are. Negative words or phrases like "cannot," "am not," or "will not" should be avoided when

creating or reciting affirmations, as it disrupts their resonance with the mind.

Think of it this way; if you are something, it's okay if you stumble and stop being that thing for a while because you know you can become it again if you work towards it. But if you promise *not* to do something, yet do it anyway through normal human error, then deep down you'll feel as if you've failed yourself. Therefore, keep affirmations positive in diction so that even if you stumble and fall, it'll be easier for you to pick yourself up again mentally.

When it comes to healing Chakras and achieving a better life, you need to have the will to keep picking yourself back up.

2. For your Root, even if it is completely blocked, you can affirm with, "My Root invites positive change as it unblocks."

Beyond that, focus your affirmations on where you feel stable or safe. Focus on your connection to your flesh and bone and affirm your faith in your ability to survive current circumstances.

3. For your Sacral, even the most blocked can affirm, "As my Sacral heals, I can create."

Beyond that, focus your affirmations on the value, care, and respect you have for both your body and its creative impulses. This includes your sexuality.

4. For your Solar Plexus, even the most blocked can affirm, "Every day my core has a chance to grow brighter."

   After this, focus on affirming that, as an adult, no one can make better life choices for you than yourself. No one can know you as intimately as you can potentially know yourself. Affirm self-respect and a recognition of your personal power. Affirm memories where you displayed strength or bravery, even if it was something as small as speaking up for someone, treating a stranger kindly, or keeping a promise despite difficulty (e.g. meeting a hectic deadline).

5. Now, your Heart. Even the most broken Heart can affirm, "I can work to rise above my pain," so that even if something always hurts, that hurt will not define you.

   Beyond that, focus affirmations on peaceful or forgiving behaviors that you can exhibit.

6. For your Throat, even the most blocked can still say, "As I balance, my words become clearer."

   Beyond that, focus on affirmations of truth, integrity, comfort in communicating feelings, and willingness to share one's wisdom.

7. Even the most blinded Third Eye still leaves room to affirm, "As I unblock, I will gain greater vision and intuition."

   From there, affirm a willingness to learn, both from your past mistakes as well as the mistakes and successes of others.

8. Your Crown, however, prefers a reverent and introspective silence when it is completely blocked. When you must speak, affirm your oneness with the world around you, among both humanity and mother nature. Affirm your presence in this very moment, or affirm your will to learn from a divine source.

Yoga

We've touched a little bit on Yoga for a few of the Chakras, but let's go deeper now. Yoga is, among other things, an ancient Tantric method of working with your Chakras, allowing movements in your body to unblock or redirect energy flow. You already know one such method for your Root called the "Downward-Facing Dog" thanks to Chapter 2, but now we shall cover at least one further method for each of your Chakras, following a progression suitable for beginners.

Don't worry about getting it perfect right away, and know that the more you practice stretching, the more flexible you'll become and the easier each pose will be for you. If you battle with a pose for one Chakra, move back to a simpler pose for another until you feel ready to work your way up again. To see meaningful benefits, it's recommended you spend at least one hour per week practicing your Yoga poses, although even a fortnightly practice is a great way to get used to things if you're alright taking things a little slow.

Root Yoga

A great way to rebalance our Root is through the "Mountain Pose." To perform it:

- Stand firm on a soft surface with feet slightly apart
- Tighten stomach, relax shoulders, point Crown skyward
- Bring your palms together in front of your Heart
- Breathe deeply, and visualize energy flowing through you from head to toe, inwards and outwards
- Visualize a red glow in your tailbone

Lunges and squats are great alternatives for fitness enthusiasts.

Sacral Yoga

Prepare for the "Revolved Triangle Pose." This pose is not suitable for pregnant women after their first trimester.

- Place your right foot forward, then turn your hips left so that the line of your pelvis is parallel to the line of your right foot
- Ensure there is a yoga block or other sturdy support adjacent to the inside of where your right foot is, and place your left hand on it. Your left hand should be in line with your face
- Place your right hand on your right hip, then slowly twist your torso to the right, taking care to keep your hips in line
- Remember to breathe
- Be aware of your pelvis and your belly as you visualize an orange light throughout that area
- Breathe
- Repeat with your lefts and rights swapped around

Once again, lunges and squats are great alternatives for fitness enthusiasts.

Yoga for the Solar Plexus

The "Boat Pose"

- Sit down, but with your soles in contact with the ground and knees bent
- Place hands behind your hips, and carefully lean backwards
- Keep the line of your head above the line of your knees

- Feel the yellow glow shine through as your core burns. For greater intensity, keep your lower legs parallel with the line of the ground.
- Hold for up to thirty seconds, and repeat up to five times

Heart Yoga

For your Heart, we'll perform what is called a "Low Lunge." To perform, begin in "Downward-Facing Dog" (see Chapter 2), then:

- Walk your right foot onto the ground between your hands, then lower your left knee so it touches the floor
- Keep your hips and shoulders parallel
- Move the tension off your hips and place your weight on your right foot. Let your left hip stretch.
- Now, lift your torso upright, with your right hand pointing upward and helping you balance while your left rests on your left upper leg
- Remember to breathe, and let your back arch backwards
- Let your mind meditate on your Heart as you maintain this pose
- After several breaths, carefully relax and repeat with your rights and lefts swapped

Throat Yoga

This one is easy. It is very similar to the meditation described earlier. However:

- While seated, ensure the tips of your thumb and index finger are in contact for each hand
- Keep your chest lifted, and your spine stretched
- Gently move your chin closer to your chest. You should feel some pressure, but do not try to choke yourself
- Chant a mantra, affirmation, or even a favorite song or speech. It can be anything, as long as it is truthful to you, and you can repeat it for between three and eleven minutes
- Do not forget to visualize this Chakra's energy as per your meditation

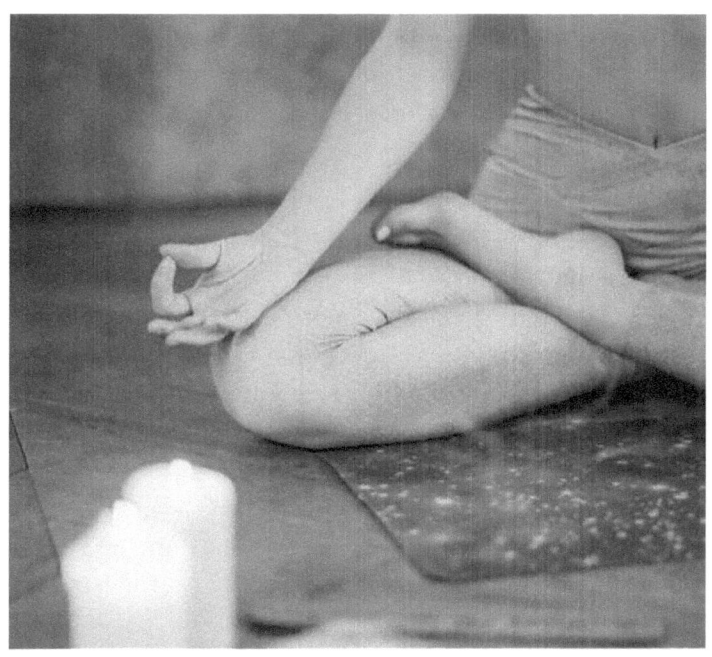

Yoga for Your Third Eye

For this, we perform the "Dolphin Pose," which encourages oxygen to circulate through our brain. To begin, assume the "Downward-Facing Dog" pose again, and then:

- Lower your forearms, so that your elbows and wrists are in firm contact with the ground
- Without lifting up your elbows, bring your palms together with your thumbs pointing toward the ceiling and the little finger on each hand pressing solidly into the floor. Keep your pelvis high.

- Gently rock forward so that your neck is hovering over your thumbs and your pelvis comes down a little, then rock back gently into your previous position, with your pelvis pointed high
- As you perform this motion, imagine a connection of energy between your hands and your Third Eye. Feel the support.
- After up to ten repetitions of this motion, release your body into a comfortable position of your choice

For a less strenuous exercise, you can instead stimulate your Third Eye by sitting as you would under Throat Yoga, but keeping one nostril blocked and focusing on breathing through your nose instead of chanting. Alternate which nostril you are blocking every few minutes. This helps the body become more aware of how it takes in breath and handles circulation.

Yoga for Your Crown

Lastly, for your Crown Chakra, we will be employing the "Butterfly Pose," a stance that requires focus, balance, and composure—a mental state that makes connecting with this Chakra far easier. Although it can be tricky to maintain, the start is not too difficult:

- Kneel down on the ground with your legs and feet side-by-side, and with your toes in flat contact with the floor

- Use your toes to lift yourself onto the balls of your feet (the collection of round parts just below the toes). Your knees should lift off the ground as you do this.
- Now, turn your feet so that the soles of your heels are in contact with one another, and open your legs as wide as possible. You can use your hands for balance as you see fit, and it's recommended that you keep your rear "seated" on your heels.
- When you feel balanced, gently join your palms together over your Heart. If you feel ready, and are confident in your fitness and balance, you can raise your joined palms above your head and hold them there.
- In this pose, undergo your energy visualization as covered under *Meditation*. It's okay if you undergo visualization faster than normal in this pose.
- After up to ten breaths in this pose, with the flow of your energy visualized, slowly release and relax

Diet

Although you likely already have good ideas regarding diet thanks to previous chapters, a general overview is included here to help you tie your thoughts and plans together, as well as include suggestions that may have been overlooked before. Consider the following foods for each Chakra:

1. Root - Vitamin C, protein, root vegetables, fiber, paprika, pepper, chives, hibiscus and rooibos tea
2. Sacral - Vitamin C, sweet fruits, citrus, vanilla, cinnamon, fresh water, tea without milk
3. Solar Plexus - Dairy, whole grains, potatoes, bananas, peas, nuts, beans, oats, cumin, turmeric, ginger, fennel, mint, chamomile, herbal teas
4. Heart - Leafy vegetables, cilantro, basil, thyme, green teas, non-acidic fruits
5. Throat - Fresh water, fruit juice (non-concentrated, no added sugars), herbal teas, blueberries, treeborne fruits
6. Third Eye - Fresh water, nuts, legumes, poppy seeds, blueberries, raspberries, blackberries, grapes, mushrooms, acai, Omega-3, dark chocolate, soy, poultry, leafy vegetables
7. Crown - Sage, juniper, frankincense, myrrh, ginger, herbal tea; your Crown Chakra also benefits from refraining from eating more than you need, and works best when the foods listed in lower Chakras are consumed in balance and moderation

Although the above foods provide a myriad of health benefits, note that there is such a thing as too much of a good thing. Although some foods may taste bitter, they should at least help you *feel* better after eating. Do not attempt to gain benefits from food you know yourself to be allergic to, and do not keep a diet if it makes you feel sluggish, dizzy, or hazy; these are signs you may be overdoing it, not only overfeeding a nutrient to your body, but also overfeeding and unbalancing the Chakra you hope to heal.

In contrast, anything that helps you feel clearer and more energetic *without* requiring constant consumption is a good choice. Whether a food does this for you or not will depend on your current health, diet, and Chakra alignment, so do not be afraid to switch up the ingredients in your eating plan every other week or so until you find what works. The above suggestions are an excellent place to begin, but only you can perfectly tailor a dietary plan to your wholly unique and sensitive situation.

Finally, note that just because you're working on your Third Eye (for example), doesn't mean you no longer need to eat food that helps your Root, it just means a higher-than-usual proportion of your diet will consist of food for your Third Eye, but still contain some supporting foods for your other Chakras. A balanced diet is good for body maintenance.

Reiki

Reiki is a form of healing originating from Japanese Buddhism that is simple in concept, but difficult in execution. As such, its inclusion is more for the sake of interest and completion. Although the original Reiki system focused on energy points known as "Tandens," modern Reiki generally opts to use the Chakra system instead. How it works is that the practitioner lays their hands on a part of your body associated with the Chakra that needs healing. The idea is that, through their touch, they bring about the transfer of energy, removing toxicities and nervous blockages while sharing their own positivity with you. Skilled practitioners know exactly which point to target in order to ease a physical or mental affliction. The process is based on knowledge and technique, however, not miracles, and requires training beyond the scope of this book.

The best place to receive Reiki is from a licensed hospital or medical clinic, as many do offer the service. If you have contact with other sources of physical therapy, such as massage, you can often ask the therapist to recommend a credible Reiki practitioner for your need. Before undergoing your first Reiki session, it also helps to ask the practitioner about their training and experience, especially if they're not working for a hospital or clinic, as unlike being a GP, you don't need special tertiary education to be allowed to practice Reiki.

Listening to the practitioner describe how they approach Reiki can help you get a feel for their character as well as how comfortable you can feel around them. If they mention the ability to ease chronic pain, rebalance your Chakras or help your biofields realign, then you've likely found the right kind of person. If they mention the ability to miraculously cure disease with their touch, however, you may wish to treat anything they say with a healthy pinch of salt from that point onward.

Overall, it's recommended that you pursue this option only after you've familiarized yourself with the previous techniques in this chapter.

Emotional Freedom Technique (EFT)

In contrast to Reiki, EFT is a form of therapy that you can easily perform on yourself, even with minimal experience. EFT works by simulating meridian responses, similarly to ASMR. Unlike ASMR, however, this reaction is triggered by touch instead of sound. When performed correctly, you'll feel a pleasurable tingling and relaxation in your head, on your face, or along your spine.

Although EFT can become complex, for the purpose of unblocking Chakras it is actually incredibly intuitive.

EFT, also known as "Tapping," involves repeated light touching with your fingertips against the parts of your body that correspond to the Chakra you wish to unblock. As you tap around that area, be sure to keep in mind a corresponding affirmation that you wish to bring into your life. It also helps to visualize the flow of energy through your body, much as you would under *Meditation,* and try to visualize how that energy branches out from the Chakra, seeing how it flows through your body, and follow your fingers along the blockages, paying attention to where your skin responds with delight and where it feels closed off. Where it feels closed off, do not be afraid to engage in a lengthy bout of light tapping on the spot, until the sensation begins to change and your energy feels as if a new channel has opened up.

Chapter 10:

Boost Your Healing - The Spiritual Guide to Crystals, Herbs and Essential Oils

Crystals and Gems

When we think of minerals, usually it's in the context of nutrients, such as salt, vitamins, or even calcium, magnesium, or zinc, all of which are vital for a strong and healthy body. However, minerals are not always for imbibing; many can be used to aid in Chakra realignment.

This is where gems come in. Although gems certainly are not edible, the unique crystal lattice that forms each kind gives them unique properties in the influence of our energy during meditation. In general principle, gems work similarly to the Emotional Freedom Technique—the exertion of light pressure on specific points to unblock pathways and create a gentle nervous system response, with the exception that the gems exert lighter yet constant pressure, while EFT is sharper but runs on a repetitive staccato. Note that you cannot just place any old gem anywhere. Each one resonates with specific parts of your body.

When meditating with gems, the first thing to be aware of is that it cannot usually be done in the normal sitting position. Each gem needs to be placed and balanced on the appropriate part, meaning you'll either need to lie down on your stomach or on your back, whichever you prefer, so that you can place the stones along your Chakra line. Aside from that, the meditation is carried out as normal.

The gems are believed to help one focus on the energy flowing through one's body, in the same way that a lightsaber seems to help the Jedi focus the flow of the Force through their body, or a wand helping a wizard focus the flow of magic. This isn't magic, of course. It's just the flow of energy.

A Rule of Thumb

When choosing gems, the general rule is to pick them according to their color, and match that color with that of each Chakra. For the Root and Crown, however, you can use black and white crystals for them respectively, in addition to the red and violet you already knew about. Finally, the Heart can benefit not only from green crystals, but also pink ones.

Additionally, note that the smoothness or roughness of a gem has little bearing on its quality or properties; whether polished and refined, or rough-hewn and ready, an amethyst is still an amethyst, a diamond is still a diamond. Focus rather on the intensity of its color, which provides you with a rough indication of the type and quality of mineral content in the gem.

For more information about specific gems that I recommend, read on.

Smoky Quartz (Root)

This is a gem that varies in color, ranging from almost clear to warm brown to even dark brown or black. This crystal is most commonly associated with your Root, and is known for its grounding properties, especially helping one mitigate any feelings of depression or anxiety during meditation that may stem from insecurity in the right to live. It's a great way to help the terminally uncertain relax when they try to center themselves.

Hematite (Root)

So-called due to its strong iron content, Hematite helps improve mental activity in matters regarding stability and security, such as finances, work ethic, basic strategy and the like. It also helps bring peace to Roots that have grown overactive, as well as help them settle down toward the end of an invigorating meditation session. Hematite can come in black, grey, silver, red, and brown colorations, with the latter two being the most common in its natural state, and is always associated with the Root.

Carnelian Agate (Sacral)

A type of Chalcedony, Carnelian Agate is placed between the groin and the navel to aid in feelings of balance, observations, and accuracy. It is most often associated with the Sacral Chakra, concentrating its benefits in one's creative aptitude, and is well known for the beautiful rusty and fiery shades of orange and red that it comes in, as well as its beautiful stripes. Unstriped variants are merely known as "Carnelian," but will still aid in healing your Sacral Chakra, helping eliminate doubts concerning the good things in one's creative output. Carnelian Agate, however, goes further by helping you unlock stores of vigor you didn't know you had, as well as aiding you on the path to free, creative, and compassionate thinking.

Gold Tiger Eye (Solar Plexus)

How fitting it is that the gemstone for your Chakra of identity looks like the eye of a tiger? In addition to banded gold, this gem also comes in banded red, black and blue/indigo variants, and all share similar properties of grounding, optimism, intuition, and awareness. Red and black variants are best for your Root, where it encourages stability, while blue/indigo variants do well for your Throat and Third Eye, boosting understanding and higher intuition respectively. However, *all* variants can work to some degree on your Solar Plexus, and the gold variant naturally excels there, helping you gain an intuitive understanding of who you are at your core during meditation, which in turn lets you more easily access the rest of the benefits that come with a balanced Solar Plexus.

Out of all variants, however, I find gold to be the best, with the other colors usually outperformed by other crystals when it comes to your Root, Throat, or Third Eye.

Rose Quartz (Heart)

Rose quartz is one of the most common crystals on Earth, and by far one of the easiest to acquire. Like most forms of quartz, trace amounts of this gem are often used in technology such as computer chips. When used in meditation, it's best placed atop your Heart Chakra, and tends to range from pale to deep pink hues. It is especially prized, despite how common it is, due to its ability to spark loving energy in the Heart, as well as have an amazingly positive knock-on effect that helps soothe all other surrounding Chakras.

Celestite (Throat)

Also known as Celestine, this crystal is a beautiful pale blue color that varies in transparency, although it is never completely opaque. In this instance, such clarity stands as a metaphor for its effects, which not only include enhanced clarity for your voice and greater harmony for your energies, but also grants positive knock-on effects to your Heart and Third Eye without even having to touch them.

Even as this gem sits on the skin at the base of your Throat (and this is where it should always sit during meditation, regardless of where you may be tempted to place it otherwise), you will feel pain in your Heart give way to love, and find the fog in your Third Eye disperse, all as you lay down and breathe. It's a potent gem that not only clears the Throat it sits on, but also helps nearby gems clear their Chakras, too. Despite the positive knock-on benefits they receive, however, never place this gem directly on your Heart or Third Eye; always assign it to your Throat, as this is where it works best.

Azurite (Third Eye)

Azurite is a beautiful blue gem known for stimulating your third eye. During meditation, it primes your brain to develop its powers of foresight, insight, and even creativity, since you'll have a better understanding of how to sync your creative output with the ebb and flow of the world around you. Azurite also helps to clear mental blocks and keep you innovative.

Amethyst (Crown)

One of the most prized crystals for meditation, this violet gem is one of the best for helping you enter the focused trance needed to conduct deep Chakra cleansing, calming the mind and dissolving basic daily insecurities to focus your consciousness on the here and now. It draws attention to your inner strength, and helps you find your inner peace in addition to acting as a guide towards your sense of spirituality. It's one of the best gems when you are unsure whether something you know is the truth or not, or even if whether it's true or not should matter to your life now. As you cannot seat this gem perfectly on your Crown while your head is lying down, either get a neck support such as a pillow to rectify this, or place the gem as close to the top of your head as you can.

Herbs and Essential Oils

Herbs have been used in healing since time immemorial. While modern medicine and operating procedures have taken the spotlight for obvious diseases and injuries, for handling the subtleties of psychological and energetic imbalance, a gentler touch is needed. Hence, herbs return into our repertoire for the purpose of realigning Chakras and performing domestic health maintenance. From herbs, we further gain essential oils (concentrated extracts of plants), whose concentration enhances nature's gift with a compelling potency.

Essential Oils

Essential oils are highly concentrated extracts of a variety of plants carrying a variety of health benefits.

Due to their potency, it is not recommended for beginners to try to apply them to children. Some individuals show allergic reactions due to the potency; if your skin reacts abrasively to a specific oil, stop using it immediately.

When purchasing oils, always ask if they've already been diluted. If they're undiluted, you should always dilute the oil before using it on your skin. You can do this by mixing one ounce of carrier medium (e.g. shea butter, cocoa butter, grapeseed oil or jojoba oil) for every twelve drops of oil. Less is more, so go slow and do not overdo it.

This mix should then be safe for use on your skin as you see fit, and should be the form in which you apply it except if instructions given for an oil below say otherwise. A good company for supplying essential oils within the US is *Rocky Mountain Oils™*.

Cedarwood (Root)

This is a pale golden yellow oil. Apply it diluted to the soles of your feet. It increases one's feeling of stability, reduces panic, and even acts as a mild aphrodisiac, which can be useful for your Sacral if applied to the rest of your body.

Rose (Sacral)

A deep red to light yellow oil, add 10-12 drops undiluted to 40 drops of Liquid Castile Soap (which you can buy online), and pour into a 1 oz. spray bottle of water. Make sure the spray nozzle has a "mist" setting. For your Sacral Chakra, mist your body before you begin your meditation (taking care to avoid your eyes and mouth). Rose aids with stress, depression, and grief, along with being an aphrodisiac, too. For the purposes of Chakra meditation, it can be substituted with clary sage, but NOT rosemary and not vice versa.

Rosemary (Solar Plexus)

Rosemary is a clear liquid. For your Solar Plexus, apply diluted to your neck, wrists, and chest. It comes alive if you engage in exercise prior to meditation and also improves memory and focus. Rosemary is excellent for solidifying identity. It also boosts circulation and soothes muscle, skin, and nerves. For Chakras, it can be substituted with cedarwood, but not vice versa.

Lavender (Heart)

A clear, yellow-tinged liquid, dilute lavender in water as with rose and spray your surroundings prior to meditation to fill the air and aid your Heart. It's sedative and allows the restful sleep that lets us get up on the right foot, reducing irritability. Lavender kills bacteria too, promoting general health. For Chakras, it can be substituted with rose, but not vice versa.

Peppermint (Throat)

Apply peppermint diluted to your throat and chest. Another clear liquid with a yellow tinge, this one is a strong stimulant and aphrodisiac. It helps reduce nausea, ease headaches, and increase alertness and overall energy, letting you come across more lively and engaging.

Clary Sage (Third Eye)

Yet another pale yellow oil, for Chakras, it can be substituted with rosemary, but NOT cedarwood and not vice versa. Apply it diluted to your forehead and temples. It's a soothing, pleasurable, amazing stress reliever that is especially potent on women. Clary sage enhances clear thought, reducing emotional obstructions.

Frankincense (Crown)

For Chakras, frankincense can be substituted with cedarwood, lavender, and rose, but not vice versa. This light yellow liquid can be applied diluted to the center of your brow, right where your Third Eye is. It promotes deep, patient breathing and relaxes the body without being a full-blown sedative. Frankincense helps ease respiratory issues.

Herbs

Dandelion Root (Root)

Sadly, dandelions are tricky to find online, but luckily they're extremely common across the globe, especially in the temperate zones of the US, Australia, and Southern Africa. Small yellow flowers with thick leafless stems, its root can be made into a tea that's excellent for healing your Root, reducing depression and easing blood pressure.

Calendula (Sacral)

This can be procured from Target, Walgreens, or Amazon. It looks similar to marigolds before being dried, and is part of the daisy family. Calendula can be used in cooking or herbal teas. It reduces sensory overload while aiding in lateral thinking.

Rosemary (Solar Plexus & Third Eye)

A common grocery store and garden herb, rosemary leaves are long and thin in proportion, but barely longer than a forefinger in scale. It's excellent for cooking, unblocks Solar Plexus energy flow, and is essential for a healthy digestive tract to boot. When ingested in herb form it helps soften one's demeanor, ease migraines, boost memory, and prevents existing "control freak" tendencies from being exacerbated.

Sage (Heart & Throat)

Another common grocery store and garden herb, sage has leaves that are a pale veridian, bumpy on one side and smooth on the other. They tend to be half the length of a finger, and nearly twice the width. Sage improves circulation, and allows you to feel safer in expressing unconditional love and other repressed emotions that are nonetheless close to your heart.

Lavender (Crown)

Beautiful, tower-shaped purple flowers atop bright green stalks, lavender has a unique and sweetly pungent aroma. It's best taken as an herbal tea, or kept intact for aromatherapy. Lavender is known for calming the body and mind, aiding in focus during meditation, as well as helping *all* your Chakras open as a side effect. It's instrumental in keeping lower Chakras spinning while you work on your highest.

Conclusion

Now, you have been equipped with all the knowledge necessary to start tending to your own Chakras. Keep using this book as a reference throughout your journey as you continue to explore the power and meaning inherent in each of your seven main Chakras. Remember, when in doubt, always return to your Root and work your way up from there. Each Chakra depends not only on those around it, but especially on those below it.

Much like how you need to study daily to excel at a subject, exercise daily to build a healthy body, or perform basic chores daily to keep a household in easy and working order, so too should you tend to your Chakras daily so that they continue to spin. Hold them as you would your children, and they will follow you spinning wherever you go. This does not mean tending to all your Chakras every day, but rather spending a few minutes working on one that looks like it's falling down a little, and giving up a small part of each day helping it back up. Employ meditation, yoga, affirmations, EFT, and the recreational activities suggested in each chapter into a routine that you're comfortable with. Look for openings in your life where you can match your activity to the needs of a Chakra; for example, dance in the morning when you first get up to help shake off the malaise of sleep, stretch your joints, as well as stimulate your Root and Sacral Chakras, reaffirming your foundation for the day. In the long run, small things like this will not only benefit you, but also everyone who knows you.

Whenever you're unsure which Chakra needs your help most, feel free to go through the questionnaire in Chapter 9 again, performing your triage. Know that while herbs, crystals, and essential oils are helpful, they are not something you need to rely on; the power is within you, and within the connections you form with life around you. Feel free to keep your diet simple, as long as it nourishes you and helps you get in touch with those deep centers of energy you carry along your spine.

No matter how many roadblocks you might encounter, no matter how much you might struggle initially, do not give up. Only in war are we discouraged to persist, but you are not fighting a war here at all. You're making friends with the energy of life residing within you. As you work your way up your Chakras, getting closer and closer to the Divine, or your ideal self, never forget that as humans we are inherently flawed, and will always have room to grow, improve, and pick ourselves back up when we fail. Do not see mastering your Chakras as a road to perfection, for you'll never arrive at that destination. No one will. Rather, let the road lead you to peace and contentment, which you will soon find plentiful as you make more room for this path less travelled.

It's been my pleasure to share this book with you. I hope I've helped you, as your support has gone a long way to helping me. I always strive to improve the value of my work, so please let both me and others know what you liked about this book; it'll give me insight into what matters to you and, if this has had any meaningful impact in your life, your review could help others find their way to that same experience.

Thank you for sitting through this part of your journey with me. I wish you all the best for your next steps.

References

Activedia. (2019). Spiritualism, Awakening, Meditation. In *Pixabay*. https://pixabay.com/photos/spiritualism-awakening-meditation-4552237/

Ahrendts, A. (2013). The Power of Human Energy [YouTube Video]. In *YouTube*. https://www.youtube.com/watch?v=mZNlN31hS78

Akin, N. (2019). Green Leaf Plant on Wooden Surface. In *Pexels*. https://www.pexels.com/photo/green-leaf-plant-on-wooden-surface-3205147/

Askinosie, H. (2015, June 9). *Chakra Stones Chart: Learn About Your 7 Chakras*. Energymuse.Com. https://www.energymuse.com/blog/chakra-stones-chart-chakra-awareness

Best Crystals. (2020). *Chakra Guide*. Best Crystals. https://bestcrystals.com/pages/chakra-guide

Breakingpic. (2015). Four Lit Tealights. In *Pexels*. https://www.pexels.com/photo/love-romantic-bath-candlelight-3188/

Corradin, S. (2014). Close-Up Photography of Marigold Flower. In *Pexels*.

https://www.pexels.com/photo/close-up-photography-of-marigold-flower-1031628/

Day, O. (2015, December 1). *How to Use Essential Oils to Balance Your Chakras*. Releaseyoga.Com. http://releaseyoga.com/blog/2015/12/01/how-to-use-essential-oils-to-deepen-your-yoga-practice

Digital Welt Magazine. (2020). *What Is Chakra Meditation? 7 Different Types of Core Chakras*. Digitalwelt. https://www.digitalwelt.org/en/lifestyle/mind-body/what-is-Chakra-meditation

Fairytale, E. (2020). Meditating With Candles and Incense. In *Pexels*. https://www.pexels.com/photo/meditating-with-candles-and-incense-3822621/

Flavio, A. (2020, April 2). *Chakra 101: An Introduction to the 7 Chakras*. YogiApprovedTM. https://www.yogiapproved.com/om/Chakra-system-introduction/

Foley, D. (2019, January 26). *Free Guided Chakra Meditation Script [PDF File Included]*. UnifyCosmos.Com. https://unifycosmos.com/chakra-meditation-script/#chakra_Meditation_Script

Freshwater, S. (2017, November 20). *1st Chakra Root Muladhara*. Spacioustherapy.Com. https://spacioustherapy.com/1st-Chakra-root-muladhara/

Geralt. (2018). Chakra, Energy Centres, Body, Center, Yoga. In *Pixabay*. https://pixabay.com/illustrations/chakra-energy-centres-body-center-3131626/

Geralt. (2019a). Chakra, Energy Centres, Body, Center, Yoga. In *Pixabay*. https://pixabay.com/illustrations/chakra-energy-centres-body-center-4354541/

Geralt. (2019b). Chakra, Energy Centres, Body, Center, Yoga. In *Pixabay*. https://pixabay.com/illustrations/chakra-energy-centres-body-center-4354547/

Geralt. (2019c). Chakra, Energy Centres, Body, Center, Yoga. In *Pixabay*. https://pixabay.com/illustrations/chakra-energy-centres-body-center-4354536/

Gorst, P. (2018, September 3). *A Brief History Of The Chakra Origin — Chakra Color Origin Myth*. Tantric Academy. https://tantricacademy.com/history-of-the-chakras/

Grabowska, K. (2020a). Close-Up Photo Of Amethyst. In *Pexels*. https://www.pexels.com/photo/close-up-photo-of-amethyst-4040585/

Grabowska, K. (2020b). Set of cosmetic bottle with pink rose on wooden plate. In *Pexels*. https://www.pexels.com/photo/set-of-cosmetic-bottle-with-pink-rose-on-wooden-plate-4041391/

Grabowska, K. (2020c). Photo Of Rose Quartz. In *Pexels*. https://www.pexels.com/photo/photo-of-rose-quartz-4040589/

Grande, M. (2018, September 13). *Essential Oils to Balance Chakras*. Medium. https://healthcareinamerica.us/essential-oils-to-balance-chakras-7a2bd1c07f78

Hairston, S. (2019, July 11). How Grief Shows Up In Your Body. WebMD. https://www.webmd.com/special-reports/grief-stages/20190711/how-grief-affects-your-body-and-mind

Heid, M. (2014, August 6). *Your Brain On: Dehydration*. Shape Magazine. https://www.shape.com/lifestyle/mind-and-body/your-brain-dehydration

Hurst, K. (2017a, September 28). *7 Chakras: What Is A Chakra? How To Balance Chakras For Beginners*. The Law Of Attraction. https://www.thelawofattraction.com/7-chakras/

Hurst, K. (2017b, October 19). *Crown Chakra Healing For Beginners: How To Open Your Crown Chakra*. The Law Of Attraction. https://www.thelawofattraction.com/crown-chakra-healing/

Hurst, K. (2017c, October 19). *Heart Chakra Healing For Beginners: How To Open Your Heart Chakra*. The Law Of Attraction. https://www.thelawofattraction.com/heart-Chakra-healing/

Hurst, K. (2017d, October 19). *Root Chakra Healing For Beginners: How To Open Your Root Chakra*. The Law Of Attraction. https://www.thelawofattraction.com/root-chakra-healing/

Hurst, K. (2017e, October 19). *Sacral Chakra Healing For Beginners: How To Open Your Sacral Chakra*. The Law Of Attraction. https://www.thelawofattraction.com/sacral-chakra-healing/

Hurst, K. (2017f, October 19). *Third Eye Chakra Healing For Beginners: How To Open Your Third Eye*. The Law Of Attraction. https://www.thelawofattraction.com/third-eye-chakra-healing/

Hurst, K. (2017g, October 19). *Throat Chakra Healing For Beginners: How To Open Your Throat Chakra*. The Law Of Attraction. https://www.thelawofattraction.com/throat-chakra-healing/

Jalan, M. (2020, July 22). *Why Does Sleep Deprivation Cause Body Ache?* Science ABC. https://www.scienceabc.com/eyeopeners/why-does-sleep-deprivation-cause-body-ache.html

King, D. (2018, March 27). *Chakra Foods for Healing & Health - Blog*. Deborahking.Com. https://deborahking.com/7-foods-to-heal-7-chakras/

Lao-Tzu, & Wing, R. L. (1997). *The tao of power: Lao Tzu's classic guide to leadership, influence and excellence* (p. 173). Thorsons.

Lomas, P. (2017a). Root, Chakra, Energy, Chi, Spiritual. In *Pixabay*. https://pixabay.com/illustrations/root-chakra-energy-chi-spiritual-2533091/

Lomas, P. (2017b). Sacral, Chakra, Energy, Chi, Spiritual. In *Pixabay*. https://pixabay.com/illustrations/sacral-chakra-energy-chi-spiritual-2533094/

Lomas, P. (2017c). Solar, Chakra, Chi, Energy, Spiritual. In *Pixabay*. https://pixabay.com/illustrations/solar-chakra-chi-energy-spiritual-2533097/

Meriwether, N. (2018, July 6). *Week 27 | Is There Scientific Proof for the Existence of Chakras? A Brief Introduction to Chakras and The Compelling Science Behind The Energy Found Within Us All*. Welltheresthis. https://www.welltheresthis.com/single-post/2018/07/05/Week-27-Is-There-Scientific-Proof-for-the-Existence-of-Chakras-A-Brief-Introduction-to-Chakras-and-The-Compelling-Science-Behind-The-Energy-Found-Within-Us-All

Mindvalley. (2019, January 25). *A Beginner's Guide To Chakra Meditation.* Mindvalley Blog. https://blog.mindvalley.com/chakra-meditation/

Moules, J. (2019, April 15). *Align Your Chakras With These 7 Chakra Yoga Poses.* YogiApprovedTM. https://www.yogiapproved.com/yoga/chakra-yoga-chakra-alignment/

New World Encyclopedia. (2015, July 15). *The Science behind CHAKRAS.* PowerThoughts Meditation Club. http://powerthoughtsmeditationclub.com/the-chakras/

Piacquadio, A. (2020). Woman Meditating In Bedroom. In *Pexels.* https://www.pexels.com/photo/woman-meditating-in-bedroom-3772612/

Pixabay. (2016a). Silhouette of Person Raising Its Hand. In *Pexels.* https://www.pexels.com/photo/backlit-balance-beach-cloud-268134/

Pixabay. (2016b). White and Purple Flower Plant on Brown Wooden Surface. In *Pexels.* https://www.pexels.com/photo/white-and-purple-flower-plant-on-brown-wooden-surface-161599/

Rankin, L. (2012). Is there scientific proof we can heal ourselves? In *YouTube.*

https://www.youtube.com/watch?v=LWQfe_fNbs

Ravier, M. (2019). Areal Photo of Sea Wave. In *Pexels*. https://www.pexels.com/photo/aerial-photo-of-big-sea-wave-3331094/

Robbins, W. (2020). *Introduction to the Chakras and Essential Oils*. Aromaweb.Com. https://www.aromaweb.com/essentialoilschakras/default.asp

Rocha, K. (2018). Black Hanging Bridge Surrounded by Green Forest Trees. In *Pexels*. https://www.pexels.com/photo/black-hanging-bridge-surrounded-by-green-forest-trees-775201/

Rocky Mountain Oils. (2018a, June 18). *Exploring Your Crown Chakra*. The RMO Blog. https://www.rockymountainoils.com/learn/exploring-your-crown-chakra/

Rocky Mountain Oils. (2018b, June 18). *Exploring Your Heart Chakra*. The RMO Blog. https://www.rockymountainoils.com/learn/exploring-your-heart-Chakra/

Rocky Mountain Oils. (2018c, June 18). *Exploring Your Sacral Chakra*. The RMO Blog. https://www.rockymountainoils.com/learn/exploring-your-sacral-chakra/

Rocky Mountain Oils. (2018d, June 18). *Exploring Your Solar Plexus Chakra*. The RMO Blog.

https://www.rockymountainoils.com/learn/exploring-your-solar-plexus-Chakra/

Rocky Mountain Oils. (2018e, June 18). *Exploring Your Third Eye Chakra*. The RMO Blog. https://www.rockymountainoils.com/learn/exploring-your-third-eye-chakra/

Rocky Mountain Oils. (2018f, June 18). *Exploring Your Throat Chakra*. The RMO Blog. https://www.rockymountainoils.com/learn/exploring-your-throat-Chakra/

Roy, G. (2014, September 26). *Healing the Seven Chakras with Herbs*. Fractal Enlightenment. https://fractalenlightenment.com/32030/spirituality/healing-the-seven-chakras-with-herbs

Sebastian, S. (2020a). *Crown Chakra - Sahasrara*. Chakra Anatomy. https://www.chakra-anatomy.com/crown-chakra.html

Sebastian, S. (2020b). *Heart Chakra - Anahata*. Chakra Anatomy. https://www.chakra-anatomy.com/heart-chakra.html

Sebastian, S. (2020c). *Solar Plexus Chakra - Manipura*. Chakra Anatomy. https://www.chakra-anatomy.com/solar-plexus-chakra.html

Sebastian, S. (2020d). *Third Eye Chakra - Ajna*. Chakra Anatomy. https://www.Chakra-anatomy.com/third-eye-chakra.html

Sebastian, S. (2020e). *Throat Chakra - Visuddha*. Chakra Anatomy. https://www.chakra-anatomy.com/throat-chakra.html

Silcox, K. (2018, December 4). *How to Use the Seven Chakras in Your Yoga Practice*. Yoga Journal. https://www.yogajournal.com/yoga-101/a-guide-to-the-chakras

Spirit Earth Awakening. (2016, December 21). *Heal The Chakras With Seven Magical Herbs!* Spirit Earth Awakening. https://www.spiritearthawakening.com/meditation/chakra-activation/heal-the-chakras-with-seven-magical-herbs

TNN. (2013, July 14). *Food for your chakras - Times of India*. The Times of India. https://timesofindia.indiatimes.com/life-style/health-fitness/diet/Food-for-your-chakras/articleshow/19661214.cms

WebMD Medical Reference. (2020). *What Is Reiki?* (M. Smith (ed.)). WebMD. https://www.webmd.com/pain-management/reiki-overview#2-5

Wise Old Sayings. (2020). *Chakra Sayings and Chakra Quotes | Wise Old Sayings*. wiseoldsayings.com. https://www.wiseoldsayings.com/chakra-quotes/

www.ingramcontent.com/pod-product-compliance
Lightning Source LLC
Chambersburg PA
CBHW030329100526
44592CB00010B/621